Trouble in the Pyrénées

(A Fat Man on the GR10)

by

William Beverley

First published in Great Britain by Schismatic Books
info@schismaticbooks.co.uk

ISBN 978-0-9933419-8-4

A copy of the British Library CIP record for this book is available
from the British Library.

Other books by the same author:

<u>Non-Fiction – Historical, Socio-Political</u>

Freedom to Fiefdom Volume One: The Descent of Man

Freedom to Fiefdom Volume Two: The Rise of the Global Predator

Freedom to Fiefdom, A Dissident's Internet Index

Making Ends Meet: Some Books to Challenge our Schismatic Society

<u>Fiction – Historical Novels</u>

Sapiens-1 The first of a Trilogy of historical novels set ca. 3000 B.C.

Colour copies of the photographs in this book may be downloaded using the following internet link:

https://drive.google.com/open?id=1oPvj1nY-8dMfiaEUvgkJPSoao9rjlkyp

If that link fails then a new one may be requested by emailing the following address with the subject line TITP-LINK.

info@FreedomToFiefdom.com

Cover Design:
Photograph – The author – Day 13: Col de la Pierre Saint-Martin.

Table of Contents

1 Prologue

This is a true story of one ill-equipped man's battle against elemental forces in the mountains – forces which at times manifested themselves as severe weather, but which were equally capable of maintaining a brooding silence.

It contains elements of humour, drama, and pathos – and there was at least one life-threatening episode in a most remote region.

On the trail and in the overnight refuges people of all sorts passed like ships in the night, sadly, never to be seen again. They were almost exclusively great memorable characters, only one or two being best forgotten.

Concerning the lower orders of animal, being beset by malicious farm dogs in the Basque country, and experiencing an unwelcome overture from a canine pest later on, made the author wary of man's best friend. This wariness gradually developed into a superstitious belief that disabled dogs, three-legged or mentally unstable ones for instance, might be harbingers of bad luck. Such nuisances should always be avoided or held at a walking pole's length.

Faced too with a concerted conspiracy by a variety of both animate and inanimate objects this account tells the tale of an inner conflict and the search for a state of grace. It's an unlikely story, but everything in it really did happen – the author has scars, photographs and a daily log to support it.

Although a little licence has, of course, been taken with some of the content of the *reveries*, even these actually happened – for which the only evidence is mental scarring.

The journey took place between May and July in the early twenty-first century, and it's a catalogue of the changes which can take place in a person during the transition from being totally unprepared and unsuited for such a venture, to a physical state of at least a modicum of fitness, and to a mental state of total self-confidence in the art of mountain trekking in all weathers.

Prologue

This account has been deliberately expressed variously in the first, second, or third person; sometimes as an account of events just past, and sometimes as if in the present – all according to the nature and context suggested by a reading of the original logbook, and based on the vivid memories it will eternally evoke.

2   To Start at the Beginning
The Reason Why

At the age of 51 and after many years sitting in front of computer screens, televisions, and the beguiling array of cask-conditioned real ale hand-pumps on the bar of my local pub, I was, I had to agree, physically challenged. This had occasionally been suggested, unkindly I thought, by a few so-called friends, and even close relatives; but I had always smiled benignly, as lazy, overweight people always do, and taken it.

Well not any longer.

I have never been particularly fit, and at six feet three, and over sixteen stones, I considered myself overweight and as soft as a good ripe Camembert cheese. There was no escaping the fact.

Compared to the weight at which I felt comfortable, many years earlier, it was like carrying around, something like twenty bags of sugar – or forty pounds; and that's not just a temporary weight on the body and soul such as the load I'd sometimes bear coming out of the local wine shop – a load in the shape of a merrily clinking bag of comfort for the weekend.

This was a burden that was there all the time. It wasn't very far off one of the large bags of potatoes from a nearby farm shop, and it was certainly more than one of the medium-sized truckles of excellent cheddar cheese that's made from unpasteurised Guernsey cow's milk a couple of miles away.

Now, I've always hated the expression couch-potato, but I was getting to be like a whole sack of them – I was digging my grave with my teeth as they say – and my whole life revolved around food and drink; people were calling me *Billy Bunter* behind my back, and the fact that we shared initials didn't help.

Having just completed about eight and a half month's commuting of six hours on the train every day (I slept most of it), in addition to the day's work as an IT contractor, I was mentally challenged as well. Some of my friends, again, might unkindly say that I had always been that way, but I'll give the first one a good kicking.

My wife, Lesley, thought that I needed a break, and who am I to disagree with her. She had just heard a radio programme about something called *The GR10 Pyrénéan trail.*

"Why not have a go at that, you could do with the exercise – and it'll take the stress away," she said. It brought to mind a remark made by the wife of Clyde Tombaugh when her husband discovered the (dwarf) Planet Pluto.

"Oh, that's nice dear."

I'm sure it was very well meant and wifely, but sometimes there is a gap between emphasis and true significance.

At the start of this adventure I hated walking, and I particularly disliked hills. If there was a chance of a lift to the pub a quarter of a mile away, then I would take it. If I absolutely had to walk, then the cosy little seaside resort of Brean Sands in Somerset was my kind of walking country. Flat, firm but comfortable underfoot, and no surprises other than an occasional worm cast to cause frustration and anger, or to threaten an otherwise peaceful training expedition. Even small blemishes in the ground underfoot, and inanimate objects of all kinds have been known to make me lose my temper.

As an example, I recall an outrageous incident several years before, when during my only attempt, ever, to paper a ceiling, I'd reached the end of one strip with some relief after a lot of thumping to make it stick. Being heavy-duty embossed paper when it started, the final flat, smooth and shiny result would anyway, have probably given more offence than a dead mouse found at the end of a carton of yoghurt. I'd just ironed the last few feet, and was just about to breathe a sigh, when I felt an ever-so-gentle tap on the back of the head, and whirling round, I found the whole strip had been stealthily detaching itself, and silently following me along the plank on which I was balanced.

Released from the last thumping, the leading edge of the strip of paper now also left the ceiling and draped itself over my head for good effect. For a very short time I was immobile, but then, with my arms flailing, and shouting obscenities, we both fell to the floor and I wrestled it like a python. My wife fled the scene and ushered our young son James from the room, lest, by this awful sight, he should become mentally challenged as well in later life.

We were pretty evenly matched, the paper and I, but I just about got the better of it, and managed to confine it to a sort of sticky, brooding, egg-shape.

It now used the well-known tactic of silence, you know the one, where your opponent refuses to respond to any sort of verbal attack. The effect that it had on me was comparable to sensory deprivation torture – the sort of set-up where you are hooded and subjected to white noise. When I recognised this *hedgehog* behaviour for what it was, I hurled it across the room and pursued it. Catching it at a disadvantage, I tore it to shreds so that it would have no chance of a second attempt, (a bit like what Seth did to Osiris), and quietly said "That'll teach you."

I refer to such shameful details and episodes merely to indicate that I'm not some sort of ascetic, spiritual or physically trained individual who might easily take to the mountains and *fit in*; and indeed, had I known about the conspiracy among animate and inanimate creatures and objects that must, even then, have been taking place some 800 miles or so away, on the high and remote Franco-Spanish frontier, then I might never have embarked on this adventure.

A Stroll on the Beach, Brean Sands and Ilfracombe U.K.

So, one weekend found Lesley and me on the way to Ilfracombe for a weekend break, a break from work that is; there was certainly going to be no break when it came to serious eating and drinking.

We'd stopped briefly at Brean Sands to investigate a caravan repair facility and, having done that, Lesley – my wife remember, the one who had suggested the ordeal – decided to take a look at the sea and the beach, and take a short walk. There was no harm in just looking I thought, and there was always the possibility of a snack and / or a beer. The car was parked just round the corner in case of emergencies, and there was a gentle breeze onto the lee shore, which, combined with a rising tide, gave a sense of security; I could approach the shoreline confident that I would not be swept out to sea and lost.

Watching the hypnotic motion of the waves I drifted into one of my reveries. If I was taken by a wave, I thought, then the slight wind, that lightest of zephyrs, should keep me fairly close into the shore, and with luck I might stay afloat until I finally made shore again at Bristol about twenty miles up the coast.

There are some good pubs and eating establishments in Bristol, the only problem would be getting dry. I was just checking that I'd got enough cash for a meal and drink at the excellent pub, *The Nova Scotia*, on one of Bristol's docks, when I was brought back to the present by Lesley. She can usually spot the tell-tale signs of my lack of attention to reality by my glazed eyes and sometimes a faint wheezing.

Thoughts of peril prompted a quick check that there was a mobile phone signal, and it seemed as though we both breathed a sigh of relief at the reassuring link with civilisation.

It was quite sunny, and in the distance I saw a dog cock its leg and pee over a child's sandcastle while the child's back was turned. I tutted and shook my head, little realising how I was to have several encounters of my own with dogs in the next few weeks, mainly in the Basque country.

Progress at Brean Sands could be measured in comfortable stages of a few hundred metres or so between simple cafés and seafood vendors – fish and chips that is. Life looked good, and I decided that the distant Pyrénées would present no difficulty if the mental approach was correct.

That night, an away-break at the Sandy Bay Hotel near Combe Martin with my wife and two old friends was a well-earned interlude during this first preparatory walk – we must have covered a good half mile that day.

The next day's walk to Ilfracombe involved more serious walking. A good five miles was achieved, with ascents and descents of anything up to 100 metres. Will the Pyrénées be as challenging I wondered?

At one point the strain was so great that during one of our 5 minute breaks – that's 5 minutes rest every 5 minutes – it took three of us to find Chris's pulse. I was about to enquire if his insurance premiums were up-to-date when a faint flutter was detected in his neck. There had been no response from other parts of his body but at least we were confident that his brain was still in good shape.

It was after this fright that we decided it would be safer to return to Sandy Bay by bus in case any of us should be overcome by exhaustion or starvation – we had, after all, eaten nothing for at least 3 hours; and then it had only been a simple full-English breakfast with all the trimmings.

Having survived this dilemma Chris revived somewhat at the mention of a crab salad, and he then suggested that the Loire (starting upstream of course) might be less mountainous than the GR10 and, overall, it might well be a more sensible route. We talked about it for a while, considering the cuisine of the area, but that alternative route was rejected – mainly on the basis of it being a predominantly *white* wine region.

We cautiously continued on to Ilfracombe; it was closer than walking back to Sandy Bay and, after recovering in a pub with a lunch of crab salad and a game of *dodge the seagull* while we ate it, the motorised retreat back to the hotel took place, and this made everyone feel much better.

Back at the hotel we found that after such a stressful morning and lunchtime we needed a nap before we could tackle dinner.

That night we had to make do with the Sandy Bay Seafood Buffet. This was a simple affair consisting of what seemed like just about the entire EEC British annual quota of crustaceans, fish, and *fruits de mer* in general. It was followed by an open season assault on a table that was creaking under the weight of an impressive display of puddings and cheeses. Definitely one in the eye for our cousins across the Channel.

Kitting Out and a Dress Rehearsal

Several visits to Cotswold Camping finally saw me equipped to follow in the footsteps of the great explorers about whom I had read in my youth: Nansen, Amundsen, Shackleton, and Scott; and more recently Feinnes. Well, maybe not Scott and his party – I didn't intend to be gone for quite as long as Captain Oates, when he uttered the famous words, "I am just going outside and may be some time." The heroic figure never came back of course.

I leave explicit details of good and bad trekking equipment to other writers. Suffice it to say that I tried to get the best and lightest gear possible – within reason. I threw a reasonable amount of money at the problem, and bought things like a titanium spoon, titanium mug, and a titanium billycan – it was actually called a kettle, although it didn't have a spout. I tried to call it a kettle but it sounded silly, so it remained a good old billycan. I almost bought an unbreakable wine glass, and I tried to find an attractive patterned cheese dish, but in the end I settled for an unbreakable coffee cafétière as a link with civilisation. I was supposed to be keeping off cheese anyway.

I also had all the essential things, like a sleeping bag and a waterproof bivvy bag, expedition clothing, maps for the whole route etc.

The packed rucksack weighed in at something over fifty pounds, and feeling a little sheepish that this is less than half of some military payloads, I staggered off for the second practice expedition of a seventeen to eighteen mile round trip to Yeovil, Somerset.

Somerset lanes in early May do not really demand an ice-pick and crampons, but it was reassuring to know they were there, just in case the weather took a turn for the worse, along with the flares, and a stout knife in case of trouble with bears. There are some woods along the route to Yeovil, but there have not been any *reported* bear incidents as far as I know. Of course, that doesn't mean they are not about, so I made sure the knife was where I could get it if it became necessary.

I also carried an old *Berocca* tube full of chilli powder. Berocca is one of the best hangover cures known to man – I've got a lot of empty tubes. I hasten to add here that my friends like them as well. Now, chilli of course is great on anything, and I reckoned that it would be good to throw in a bear's eyes if I was attacked. If I was not attacked then I would eat the chilli powder during normal mealtimes anyway – a sort of no-loss insurance premium. I liked that idea.

I was therefore well-armed and well-provisioned for any eventuality – I'd added an apple and three small bananas to the load – and I covered the first two or three miles without a rest, just reaching the brow of a hill the other side of the village of Sandford Orcas. This was tough-going, and the tarmac road surface was a little uneven in places. Somebody should write to the council I thought, there was the potential for a twisted ankle here.

I was getting tired and needed a small break from the rucksack that was beginning to feel heavy, so, at the small village of Trent I sat on the small parapet of a small bridge and ate a small banana to recover from the small ordeal so far. Everything seemed very small all of a sudden, I thought curiously and, as I relaxed, I drifted into another one of my reveries.

That's what was happening, I could see it clearly now. I was shrinking, and the rucksack was getting bigger, as if it wasn't big enough already. In my mind it was swelling in size, and it was just getting about as big as a house when I fell off the parapet, and clawed at a strap on the rucksack as I plummeted slowly past it, giving a long drawn out *"aaaaaarrrrh"* – like someone falling over a precipice. Swinging round on the strap I pulled it over and it crushed me.

I snapped out of this day-mare with a start and a furtive look round to see if anyone had noticed that I'd broken out into a sweat. I had to make sure this sort of thing was under control without assistance from Lesley, after all she wasn't going to the GR10 with me. I stole a sideways glance at the rucksack and it did look big, but probably no bigger than when I started. It was of course actually lighter by one banana's worth.

Shortly after this point the highest part of the trek was reached – the Col de Over Compton, and from here the terracotta roofs and attractive garrets and spires of sleepy Yeovil came into view. I was leaving the wilderness behind.

To Start at the Beginning

In Yeovil I bought a camera, over-trousers, and finally, after much searching, an acceptable type of hat that fitted. People were turning to look at me, and I felt a bit self-conscious in the hat. I realised later that I'd completely forgotten the ice-pick and crampons that were strapped to the back of the rucksack, and I wondered if I should make for the artificial ski slope where I might blend into the background better. Unfortunately this ploy had to be abandoned when I remembered that it had ceased trading some years earlier.

The return journey was exhausting, and it was during this half of the expedition that I first realised that the rucksack was haunted. On hearing small clinks, rattlings, scrabblings and movements from behind, I twisted round several times only to see the open road. The only explanation was that the ethereal companion was actually *in* the sac. This phenomenon recurred many times in the Pyrénées and, even after a change of sack, there was still evidence of some small poltergeist activity in the form of occasional rattles and knocks.

The re-ascent of the climb to Over Compton was a nightmare with stops every ten or twenty yards, and I only just made the summit.

After five more agonising miles I finally staggered into the house, thankful to be alive and with serious doubts. I was knackered.

The pack had to be reduced in weight, and I called in my advisers, Terry and Les. These are fairly serious walkers and they were in a state of great excitation and envy that I was going on such a trip without them. First to go in an effort to lighten the load were the crampons and ice-pick and, apart from one or two literally life-threatening days, this was a good move. I received a look of disbelief when I laid out my catapult and heavy steel ammunition that I'd been intending to use to hunt rabbits for food. I have to admit it was quite heavy, and in the event I didn't see a single rabbit anyway.

Next to go was my plastic coffee cafétière. I couldn't understand why my friends thought it was a ridiculous inclusion in the first place. The image of fresh coffee by a campfire at night or morning was compelling, and for one or two days I tried to sneak it back into the pack until Terry hid it so I couldn't take it. Then my spare gas canister went, followed by my water purification pump. The pump was only based on iodine crystals, and liquid iodine which I also had is more versatile. Sections of the manuals for my camera and expedition watch / altimeter in various foreign languages were considered to be superfluous, and, together with numerous other items that had originally seemed indispensable, they all went back into my expedition trunk.

Weighing in again, I was pleasantly surprised to find that we'd reduced the load by about ten pounds from fifty or so down to about forty. Looking back on it, thirty to thirty five pounds would be a really comfortable pack.

Apart from a couple of three mile jaunts, my preparations were complete, and I was getting fidgety to begin.

Into the Abyss, the Journey to Base Camp

Lesley and I stayed with our friends Terry and Suzanna in Surrey for my last day and night before leaving the U.K. for the unknown, and when the day of departure arrived I caught the train from Stoke d'Abernon to Waterloo. With cropped hair I looked like something which should be confined in an enclosure reinforced with strong mesh – or at least like a person who belonged in either Alcatraz or the French Foreign Legion.

Hovering on a razor-thin edge of indecision I waved goodbye to Lesley; and Terry, like a prison warder, escorted me part of the way to where he could get another train from Clapham Junction. I then continued alone into Waterloo and felt as though I was setting out for an appointment with Jack Ketch, the notorious seventeenth century executioner at Lincoln's Inn Fields and Tyburn.

A cheap day return Eurostar ticket between Waterloo and Paris was something like ten or twenty pounds cheaper than a single ticket. That makes no sense to me, so, although I didn't want to come back quite that quickly – at the moment that is – I asked for the cheaper ticket. I was not aware of any reason why I should not do that, and the ticket tout attempted to sell me one. However, at this most critical time higher forces in the form of *The Computer* took an interest, and the tout told me I could not have my chosen ticket because there were no seats available on any return trip that day.

After fleetingly thinking that this could be the excuse I needed to cancel the entire enterprise I told him that I didn't mind if there were no seats – I could always stand – whereupon he batted his eyelids and said that he personally didn't mind either. He then leaned forward with his head tilted slightly and with one eyebrow raised, and announced that – *The Computer* did mind.

It would not let me have the ticket and that was final.

So because there were no return seats this meant that I was paying extra for a one-way outward seat on the same train as people who were going to get two trips for their money – for less money in fact.

I couldn't let this rest so I went further – I was getting worked up.

"If the return seats balanced as implied, but I'm going one way only," I argued, "then it might also be an extremely worrying indication that more people are leaving the country than are entering it – the country is slowly but surely being deserted." I watched while he considered the arguable logic of this, but I followed up before he could fabricate a response.

"We might have a real problem in a few weeks," I explained, "the streets would all be empty, the power would fail, and the ticket machine will stop working."

I paused while he took this in.

"What will you do then?" I demanded.

He continued to look blankly at me.

"Eh my good fellow! Heavens above, even *The Computer* will be silenced! Now be a good fellow and let me have the ticket before all the lights go out as they surely will."

I should add here, that during a hypothetical proposition, especially a dodgy one, the subtle shift from *would* to *will* mid-sentence can often go unnoticed. (I bet you, the reader, didn't spot it.) The recipient becomes convinced of the truth of the hypothesis and, if it's gloomy enough, you have them. I tried to work this trick on him twice but he clearly was not having any of it. Neither did my explanations that I did not mind paying less get anywhere; they were greeted with an anglicised version of the Gallic shrug and the excuse that it was *the system*. I would like to have the opportunity to try bribing *The Computer* with its preferred currency – volts – lots of them.

Lastly, I advised him to buy a ticket quickly before there was no-one left to sell him one, after which I left, satisfied that I'd made a point but a little worried that my argument might be true. I had to forcibly stop myself trying to judge the nett flow of people in and out of the station concourse.

The combined remaining journey, across Paris from Paris-Nord to Paris-Montparnasse, and then from Paris-Montparnasse to Hendaye was about half the cost of the journey from Waterloo to Paris, and yet two to three times further. I wasn't surprised that the U.K. would be empty before I got back, at those prices you couldn't afford to stay.

Unfortunately, the only available seats on the French train going south, were in a smoking carriage – a dispensation eagerly taken up by most of the travellers.

Hendaye was the destination because it was the official start of the GR10 coast to coast walk – the 500 to 600 mile trek between the Atlantic and the Mediterranean. Other railheads can be found at Biarritz and Saint-Jean-de-Luz, but they still leave the walker short of the real starting point, and requiring another train or bus.

Stumbling from the train at 11:30 p.m. on the southwest outskirts of Hendaye with no idea of accommodation prospects was something that I told myself would be a good test of initiative. I could always make for the beach and use my bivvy gear. However, seeing some neon lights just across the road from the station was a definite clue and, bolting for the nearest bar, La Palombe Breve, was a definite pass to this test since they also provided a room for the night.

Completing the log for today's journey, I decided that tomorrow would become Day One, and so, on this Day Zero, I turned in and wondered what tomorrow would be like.

3   Pays Basque Ouest, Pyrénées-Atlantiques
     Day 1: Hendaye Plage to Biriatou
     10:15 – 13:45

Morning Anxiety is my term for a sense of unease that besets one on waking. The slow, and sometimes not so slow, realisation that life has not changed significantly overnight, and that yesterday's horrors are still there. At other times the horrors are non-existent and may just be the fading remnants of a disturbing dream. Such brief anxiety on waking is something that many people feel during periods of stress or challenge. These horrors usually take on a completely disproportionate significance during those first few minutes of returning consciousness.

I get it even when I'm not challenged. I get it on holiday. In fact I get it when I'm wide awake for goodness sake.

Well, I had a serious bout of *Morning Anxiety* when I awoke that first morning in Hendaye. I peeled back one eyelid and glanced around the room. The shuttered windows mercilessly admitted just enough light to penetrate the drab gauzy curtains, and reveal the circumstances of my confinement.

The utilitarian furniture was still all there, exactly where it was last night.

On one side there was a shabby and scratched dark brown chest of drawers – no doubt with yellowed, old newspapers lining the drawers. It had a top which was decorated with burn marks – quite likely the last vengeful acts of a neglected Gauloise. Opposing the chest of drawers there stood an unusually small (by French standards) mock-walnut wardrobe with doors that didn't quite stay closed, and this was flanked by a wash stand with a top of slightly chipped reddish brown marble – minus the traditional porcelain jug and bowl. Crouching on the edge of the frayed carpet – it was in a sort of no-man's land – a decrepit carver chair with arthritically twisted and misaligned legs was humbly presenting my clothes like an old butler.

In the corner was a small cracked wash-basin. This was fed by pipes that had been so heavily painted, they didn't really need any copper to contain the abysmally low pressure water, which, over decades perhaps, had managed to escape in a slow drip from one of the ancient taps. The prolonged dribble had left a brown stain down one side of the basin.

The whole scene was encased in wallpaper that was as old as a really good Calvados cider brandy, and pretty much the same colour in places. Like the French nation, it was probably beginning to lose its original colour when Hitler was riding triumphantly through Paris in 1940. If he'd known about that wallpaper, I thought, it might be why he never came here – the Hôtel that is – he did actually visit Generalísimo Franco, who popped over from Spain, at Hendaye railway station in October of that year.

It occurred to me that being in this room was like being inside a wrapped booby-prize, and I was the booby.

And then there was me, reflected in an old mirror, mottled and browning in places like an old person's skin – the mirror that is, not me. I was as smooth as a babies bottom and as white as a sheet of A4 printer paper, a ream of which I did not want to see for a long time.

With only one eye open, the other one was stuck closed, everything looked flat and featureless, without depth; and I thought maybe I could reach out and erase it all with a wave, make it all go away. I shut the eye, and, with an effort, opened the other one to see if I could get a different impression. Nope, the room was still the same. I swivelled it upwards and looked at a brown water (I hope) stain on the ceiling, swivelled it down to the worn candlewick bed-cover, decided things were getting worse not better, and closed that one as well.

Feeling depressed and hung-over (which I wasn't) I took a deep breath, and defiantly opened both of them. Like a leopard going for the kill the room leaped into relief and focus and, with horror, I spotted my Pyrénéan Guide-book propped against the faded floral curtains. I immediately realised where I was and had a small panic attack.

Someone must have put that book like that on purpose, I thought, and I looked around the shadowy room to spot the culprit. The door was locked however, and I was alone. I decided that they must have gone out by the half open window from which they could then have dropped down into the alley below. I bet it was the ticket tout from Waterloo trying to get his own back. So, he'd believed my gag about Britain being empty before Christmas after all, and he'd followed me here. The crafty bugger was obviously a master at keeping a straight face. I wouldn't want to play Poker with him. In fact I can't even play Poker, never could understand the rules, so I didn't really want to play anyone at it.

It was then that I remembered or *broke* the dream, as they say, that I'd been having when I awoke. I'd been having a nightmare that I'd gone to the Pyrénées to do a 600 mile walk and I'd been desperate to wake up. Now that I had woken up I was desperate to go back to sleep again and try modifying the nightmare. Maybe I might make it a bit shorter and somewhere else – *Brean Sands perhaps, or even the horrifying terrain around Ilfracombe will do*, I crooned to myself mentally. With a start, I spotted that silver-tongued use of *will*, and I realised that even I wasn't being taken in by it. It was clear that there was no going back.

At this low point I bit the candlewick bedspread hard in revenge. Fortunately it was nearer than any of my own possessions, and less likely to damage my teeth.

I then got out of bed to look out the window in case the ticket tout was still within range of a shot with a cracked blue vase of dusty plastic flowers which was on the wash stand. I think they were daffodils – or *jonquils* as the French call them – but whatever they were it was fruitless, he was completely out of sight. He was probably half-way back to Waterloo station in London by now – if he managed to get a return ticket that is.

Dressed, washed, outside by about 07:30 at La Gare, Hendaye Ville!

Let's get the pronunciation of Hendaye right before we go any further. The *H* is silent and it's pronounced as are the two English words *on* and *dye*. When I first thought of this representation, I felt there was something intimidating or foreboding about it, but I couldn't exactly put my finger on it. Of course if it's taken as two commands, then it's not the best way to start an expedition. On! Die!

La Gare, the railway station, is not the start point of the GR10 and, as a matter of principle rather than any sort of common sense, I was not prepared to compromise at this point in the adventure. Maybe later I thought, but not now anyway. So do I walk or get a taxi to the real start point at the casino in the town? I decided to walk and, after only a few metres on my first day, I had the first undesirable experience. Apart, that is, from having started in the first place.

I came across a man shouting at cars and also at a fat lady who was waddling down the road in front of him.

"Cochaine!" he shouted hoarsely at the top of his voice – I interpreted that as *sow*, or maybe *Mrs. Pig* – and every few seconds he gave a twitch or shake of his head. She held her own, looking round once or twice and calling him something unprintable.

After about fifty metres she dived into a house, turned and bellowed something else at him, and slammed the door. He looked like a little weasel – a rattish and thin-faced Rasputin type of character, with a huge nose, and with a wispy moustache and beard – something like that of English King Charles I. He wore a poncho and a brown felt hat, and he was carrying a hold-all, in which I imagined he was carrying body parts, fat human ones; and as he walked he was leaning slightly forward and intently casting his head from side to side as if he was after a scent; more body parts maybe.

The pantomime was being played out on the other side of the road, and when I saw the *Cochaine* wasn't going to be physically attacked I walked on but stopped to take a photograph of a railway siding, still within sight of the Gare. I don't know what I would have done if she'd actually been attacked, but it didn't seem right to just ignore it, though that is what I really wanted to do, like everyone else who was on the street at that time. The abuser (now on my side of the road) ignored me and disappeared into the distance shouting at more cars and *cochaines*. He seemed equally partial to animate and inanimate objects.

What I took to be my first ever sight of Tourette's syndrome in operation was not a happy introduction to the GR10. Why did it have to happen at all, let alone here and today?

I walked the two miles or so to the sea-front area without further incident, and on the way I passed a junction where I saw my first *ballise* (footpath marker). It was a place to which, I noted, I would have to return. I had some difficulty finding the casino and actually walked past the real start point without realising it.

I bought cash, postcards, raisins, peanuts – and dates.

Laurie Lee, the author of *As I Walked Out One Midsummer Morning*, had carried dates during his epic journey through Spain in 1935 at the time of the run-up to the Spanish Civil War, so I thought this was a sensible move and that it put me in good, if posthumous, company.

I ended up carrying the blasted peanuts (it was a stupidly big bag, about half a kilo) for some fifty or sixty miles before I threw them away untouched.

The tide was going out, and I therefore had a long trek over the sand to put both hands in the Atlantic, after which I walked due south from the sea, using my compass so I wouldn't get out of my depth, towards a white obelisk on the promenade; it looked a bit like Cleopatra's Needle on the London Embankment.

With the casino behind me, the wrong one I subsequently realised, off I went. I wasn't particularly concerned about this, since I'd passed the other casino anyway, but it would have been satisfying to have *consciously* acknowledged the sign that I have been told exists at the start. Perhaps I'll go back and do it again.

As I walked eastwards along the promenade in Hendaye, alongside some well-kept gardens, I passed a sweeping machine being driven by a man, and escorted by another man some yards in front who was carrying a running chainsaw but doing nothing with it. I was at first baffled by this, but it turned out to be not a chainsaw at all, but a leaf blower to get leaves out of corners ready for the sweeper. The trouble was, it was very windy, and by the time the sweeper arrived all the leaves were safely back in their corner. It seemed futile, and at the time I wondered if my attempt on the GR10 would also turn out so.

Further on through the town, just as the road climbed towards the outskirts, an elderly lady came up to me and simply said, "Quelle courage."

I looked round to see if she was speaking to someone else, but she'd addressed me. I felt slightly proud and humbled at the same time, and she disappeared into the distance shaking her head.

I got lost leaving Hendaye – ignominious – but the signs in the town were not obvious, and I subsequently considered that I was probably not yet attentive enough or tuned to the task. I knew very well that I was not on the exact trail, but I also knew roughly the direction of the necessary recovery plan. I eventually had a horrible trek on roads to attempt this route recovery, and in the belief that water would be plentiful during this stage, I'd started with less than half a tank. My capacity was two and a half litres, and at the start of all later stages I made sure that this was filled – heavy but satisfying to know that it was always available.

Going by compass and guesswork I was beginning to get a little annoyed at my failure to keep to the route so early on the first day, and, although I wasn't overly concerned, as soon as I saw a group of workers I thought I was saved.

I'd stumbled across a road construction crew spreading tarmac, and among their number was a surveyor – bristling with surveying equipment, an electronic compass, and with a theodolite included in his armoury. It turned out that there were two of them in fact. These people would certainly be able to tell me exactly where I was, I thought. I opened my map, and asked them if they could confirm precisely where on the map we all were. I said I thought I was – there – pointing just off a road junction. The older surveyor pushed his hat further back on his head, and then they both scratched their heads in the same slow fashion, and announced that they hadn't a clue. I found I had an urge to scratch my head as well, and just look at them in case it might provoke some dim memory of where we all were. I've no idea where they thought they were taking the road, or how they even got where they were.

While I was studying my map at another road junction a mile or so further on, a lady stopped her car to ask if I was *perdu* – lost. Not wishing to appear a complete idiot I said, "Peut-être Madame," meaning perhaps. She found this oxymoron quite amusing and immediately broke into

English. Why do they always do that? She confirmed that I was indeed where I had – *peut-être* – thought I was, and I then asked her in French if I could buy or find water nearby. To my great relief and gratitude she gave me a bottle of water from the seat of her car – an angel of mercy. She was the manageress of a garden centre at the road junction, and I said I would revisit some day. I made a mental note that I had to carry more water.

Very shortly after this I got a view down into a wide valley, and I could see what could only be the A63 below, with heavy goods vehicles queuing at the frontier. My only problem was that I was several hundred metres too far north, still, a bit of a detour to the south from where I was should put me right.

I regained the GR10 quite quickly after this and I continued to follow the, by now fairly clear, track over the RN10 road (*Route National*), and under the wider A63 road (*Autoroute*). It was all at this stage unimpressive, and being early in the adventure, I found it pretty tiring. If I had trained as hard as was sensibly required, then this would have been a stroll. As it was, a combination of water shortage, and lack of fitness was a bad start.

When I got to Biriatou I was totally knackered, and I drank copious amounts of brown water from a pump in the village square. I then searched for the Hôtel that I believed and prayed was here. I ached. Everything ached – my feet, legs, back, shoulders and arms. Even my face, teeth and hair ached. I was only later, after a few more days, to realise why my teeth ached so much. To be on the safe side, I'd had a check-up with my dentist only a couple of weeks earlier, and this dull ache seemed recent.

My first day had been about twelve and a half miles including the perambulations in Hendaye. The stroll to Biriatou should have taken about two and a half hours, and certainly does not constitute a one day stage. I loafed around for the rest of the afternoon in a daze, occasionally glancing fearfully at the brown hillside and ridge to the east that was tomorrow's challenge.

The Hôtel Bakea, when they eventually let me in, was a luxury. I had a beer to start, and although the food was good, with the accommodation cost, it was ridiculously expensive. As part of what might well turn out to be a three month trip, that daily cost would blow the budget by next month.

During the meal a recording of some Andean pipes was playing in the background. The tune was one of the theme tunes from the *Watch With Mother* children's television programme – *Andy Pandy* from the 1950s. It was Looby Loo's theme tune which began with the words, *Here we go Looby Loo....*, but in this case it was played very slowly and eerily on those follicle-stimulating pipes. I couldn't believe I was hearing that tune in this location. I didn't even expect it to be known outside of a BBC television children's programme circle, though it is in fact a fairly well-known international English language nursery rhyme.

Everything suddenly seemed surreal as I suspiciously watched the brooding, massive uplift of the Pyrénéan foothills that waited for me about half a mile away. I ploughed through intentionally cold soup, Salade Champêtre – a sort of luxury *paysanne* or peasant's salad – milk-fed lamb, Badoit mineral water, and a final Calva in an effort to feel that I was on holiday. I hadn't ordered it, but I was told the cold soup was free; I think they were trying to get rid of it. I never did like cold soup.

I went to bed early and drifted towards sleep with an advanced case of morning anxiety already beginning, but before I finally took up that nocturnal, almost foetal position that most of us adopt in bed, the surreal and haunting Andean pipes went through my head and made me think of how much closer I now was to the spirit of place that has driven some of my favourite eccentrics – such as Dali, Cézanne, and Miro – to create their masterpieces.

I had a vision of the charismatic Looby, and wondered what effect the sublime spirit of the mountains might have on an impressionable innocent like me.

The GR10 and the Pyrénées are not just a physical magnificence, they are a formidable life, and mind-altering influence.

Day 2: Biriatou to Olhette
08:30 – 18:30

What a beast of a day, I was totally knackered again when I reached the day's objective. This stage, it is really only part of a stage, should have taken about four and a half hours, not ten.

As I was leaving Biriatou I looked back and saw a group of soldiers milling about. They were getting in and out, and fussing around their covered transport. It looked as though they were assembling their kit for an exercise run up the hills. I'd already climbed about 150 metres according to my altimeter, and I was recovering, basking in the glorious and still early sun. I was leaning on a gate, and was marginally less beetroot-faced than I'd been five minutes earlier. Letting my mind wander, I became a fugitive during the Peninsula Wars, and the heavily-armed French Militia below were after me. As the first platoon ran up the hill I was tempted to hide, and only just snapped out of the reverie in time. The group of about eight, khaki-clad, and similarly beetroot-faced (I was pleased to see) soldiers rushed past without any obvious sign of hostilities – were they trying to surround me I wondered. I noticed that they appeared to be unarmed, although they had small packs that probably contained some hideous nerve agent. Then it occurred to me that the chilli powder was not easily to hand. Furthermore, the knife was at the bottom of the rucksack. It will be just my luck to run into a platoon of bears as well now, I thought miserably.

While this first mock assault was taking place – for that's clearly what it was, a diversionary tactic to put me off my guard – I'd moved away from the gate to give myself some space to manoeuvre. A second group – another eight or so – suddenly arrived without warning where I'd been standing only a few minutes earlier, *phew*, that was close. I could tell they were not happy about the plan of attack – or the route. They stopped a few metres away and held a conference that resulted in the recall of the first group, at which point there was an animated discussion with much hand-waving. I took this as a sign of surrender and began trying to work out how I could get them all back to Waterloo as prisoners. I had just decided that I might have to kill one or two as an example, when it became obvious that although they were not exactly lost (*peut-être* came to mind), they were clearly unhappy about the GR10. I knew how they felt.

I casually strolled over and, holding out my map and compass with a smile, asked where they wanted to go and if I could be of any assistance. (The nice guy first, then they'll get the nasty guy – with the hot chilli and cold steel). This was taken with a sense of humour in the way it was intended, and the whole battalion had a good laugh about the incident.

I had intended to announce that I'd see their commanding officer to accept his sword in token of complete and unconditional surrender. My next move would have been to count them all to make sure there was no cheating, and to then let them know that they would all have to make their own way to Waterloo under parole because I hadn't been able to get even one return ticket.

Before I could get a cable-tie on even one of the blighters however, they about-turned and ran off down another track. I think they'd even got a couple of tanks behind the church as well. I wanted to shout cowards after them but all that came out was *jonquils* – daffodils. I didn't see them again, and I decided they were probably with the French road crew that seemed equally lost.

I reached the Col d'Osin at 374 metres without any real effort, and enjoyed the rolling foothills and easy walking on grass.

Further on, the Col d'Ibardin was full of plant pots and Basque underwear shops; a strange combination, and awful commercialisation. I bought two litres of water – I'd started with two litres but had already finished that. I looked enviously at people in groups in restaurants. I watched them leaving, smiling, arm in arm, to their cars, no doubt on their way back to a comfortable hotel and an afternoon nap, or even afternoon tea. I was alone, and faced with discomfort, privation, and no-one to talk to or share the misery.

Everything after this was a dreadful slog. It was no real distance at all, but walking all remaining stages today was awful – why was I here? When would it end? The sound of cow bells is very atmospheric but I could have one of those hanging from a tree in the back garden at home, and whenever there was a breeze I could close my eyes and be back in the Pyrénées without the hassle.

After a mixture of short walks, and longer and longer rests, I thankfully crawled the last few hundred metres along the descending and tree-lined path, into the sleepy hamlet of Olhette, and arrived at my first gîte d'étape. The kind considerate guardienne / farmer's wife said something in French which might be roughly translated as follows.

"*Aaaaah*, you do look red and tired, take a nap, then come and see about dinner."

She was exactly right about the appearance.

The dormitory was excellent, hot water was excellent, and so, showered, and after washing shirt and socks, a nap was indeed just right. What was to turn out to be an excellent meal along with the fine accommodation – demi-pension for FFr 180 – seemed very good value, and I decided that paying cash would also lighten the load.

So, much refreshed after the shower, I adjourned to the farmhouse for the evening meal. At first there was some sweet beer that made me think of a draught beer shandy. This was quickly followed by vegetable soup, lots of bread, and a carafe of red wine. I took a timed, self-photograph at this auspicious moment, and wondered what would be next. In short order she appeared with rice, sweetcorn, cucumber and a hothouse-worth of tomato, all languishing beneath a layer of mayonnaise. It was real, and very good fodder, but far too much. I had just decided that I'd done sufficient damage to the meal to indicate great approval and avoid any offence, and I was just entering an after-dinner trance, when the very pleasant farmer's wife, who administered this oasis, approached so silently as to make me jump. She stood quite solemnly before me with a huge platter that just about accommodated an enormous and very dignified black pudding or sausage. She didn't say anything at first, and I was blinking and smiling like a buffoon, first at the sausage and then at her, when she asked me if I liked it. I knew that there was a right and a wrong answer here, so, obsequious creature that I am, I replied that it was possibly the most handsome black pudding that I had ever seen, and that if I had a first-prize rosette with me,

I would have had no hesitation in pinning it on the awesome creature. I think I referred to it as a *bête* i.e. beast, and hoped that this would not be taken as an insult. I supposed that she was really asking me if I *would* like it, but French verb declensions always did seem a bit obscure.

She smiled at either my humour or my poor French, and left the room. Now at this point it still was not entirely clear to me whether she was just proud of the sausage and wanted me to share its glory, or whether she really was going to cook the beast and present me with it, so I stayed where I was, and waited expectantly.

From where I sat, the view through the open door was spectacular – a huge Pyrénéan ridge, golden in places as the sun went down, and backed by a deepening blue sky. The evening air was now clear and warm without being too oppressive. There were various shades of green and brown stretching towards the rocky outcrops that lined the ridge, and buzzards were circling high above, and making their characteristic high-pitched piping sound. The dining-room was a typical farmhouse living-room, flagged floors, exposed beams, a cheese press in one corner, enormous Armoire (wardrobe) against a wall, and in another corner a grandfather clock casing, sadly with no innards. A flight of stairs went directly from the room to an upper level, from where there were occasional sounds of young Basquelings.

After I'd enjoyed about 15 minutes of such contemplation, the farmer's wife entered with a tray of real chips made from home-grown potatoes and, of course, the anticipated black pudding. So much for the *régime* – diet in English. I felt a cad not eating everything, but complemented her on the delicious black pudding – the *bête*. I had to stop her at the apple and yoghurt stage, and I'm convinced that there would have been a cheese course if I had survived.

I had met a sixty-ish man on the trail that day – he'd lived all his life in Hendaye, and had done the complete GR10 in 1987. He and his dog walked with me for a few kilometres through some woods before they branched off to return to Hendaye. I realised it was comforting to walk in company.

During today's walk I took a ten minute break every hour, rucksack off. The water lasted better this day, though I'd bought an additional two litres at the Col d'Ibardin, and had been obliged to make a reserve with a drop of iodine at a healthy looking stream.

I seem to be stopping every fifty metres on any uphill gradient. I'm now learning to spot the GR10 markers or *ballises* as they are called – a band of white over a band of red. I once got confused when I saw a cross formation, but realised that this meant *not* the GR10. I had clearly not done enough homework.

Overall the way was much better marked today. Tomorrow's initial ascent looks worse than anything so far – unrelenting up for about two kilometres – and steep – I shall probably have a nightmare tonight.

All alone in the bunkhouse – there are no locks on doors, and no curtains – I chose a defensible bunk positioned in a corner, and kept my walking poles and knife close at hand in case of attack by bears, intruders, or any other phantom of the night. It had been a mixed blessing to bring Bill Bryson's book *Walk In The Woods* to read at night. This was a tale of mixed fortunes on the Appalachian Trail in America and, although while reading it I could escape from the reality of my current situation, when I put the book down I found that my imagination, which doesn't really need a lot of encouragement, had been stoked to new horrifying levels of activity.

Pays Basque Ouest, Pyrénées-Atlantiques

Day 3: Olhette to Sare
09:00 – 16:00

This was the stage when the marching songs kicked in. I have no idea why this happened, although the lyrics may have been prompted by one or two incidents during the last couple of days. The first unbidden companion went to the tune of a well-known Grenadier marching song, the sort of thing that would be accompanied by a Souza band:

"All of a sudden a bloody great pudding came flying through the air,
Well it missed me mam but it hit me dad and it knocked him off his chair.
Then, me granny went crackers she stood on his knackers and pissed against
the wall...,
So after that, we all fell flat, so she couldn't see us at all."

Chorus :
"And we all had a real good tiiiiiiime...,
We stood in a liiiiiiine...,
And did it in rhyyyyyyme...,
And we all had a real good tiiiiiiime...,
That's how you get to SAAAAAARE..."

The name of the village, Sare in this case, would be drawn out and shouted with vigour, and this slot in the verse would, on later stages, be replaced by the name of the then current objective. The whole rhyme would be endlessly uttered like a mantra, sometimes silently, and sometimes I would sing it out loud. I couldn't suppress it however hard I tried. I felt as though I was going mad, and I began to hate walking, mountains, and particularly the Pyrénées.

The next distraction went to the tune of the well-known *Gay Gordons* of farmyard ceilidh and folk dance fame:

"We've got hens in our back yard, we feed 'em on Indian corn,
And some lay eggs, and some lay bricks,
The rest we chuck over the wall."

Chorus: (shouted):
Auntie Mary, had a canary down the leg of her drawers,
When she farted, it departed, to a round of applause."

This tune also went through my mind, and became a marching song when I felt aggressive enough.

The final unstoppable companion was the Andean Pipe rendition from Biriatou – the ghastly *Andy Pandy* theme from *Watch With Mother* that I'd seen many times when about four or five years old.

Any one of these tunes would go through my mind in time to the rate of walking, climbing, staggering or lurching that seemed appropriate to the terrain. They could all be adapted to any given pace. So, with this latest addition to the mental baggage, I went into the stage – 580 metres over the Col des Trois Fontaines just below La Rhune.

On leaving the gîte d'étape at Olhette, I heard a donkey in a neighbouring field kicking up a tremendous fuss, and turning to look at it, I was greeted by a diabolically grinning piebald face – ears flat, teeth bared, and head slightly thrown back. The beast was clearly in hysterics and I was the only obvious cause. I glared at it, looked around to see if anyone was watching, and gave it my best donkey impression back. I can do a pretty good donkey impression, and it shut up and pricked up its ears.

Stopping to consider this *Devil's Parody* and the possible reason for hilarity, I found that I could not remember packing two small straps – not a particularly life threatening omission, but such carelessness could be the start of a more worrying rot. I went back to the previous night's bunk and found that the two straps had slipped down behind the mattress, and although I'd peered beneath the bed – a habit I repeated every morning of the expedition – I had failed to spot them.

Starting again, I nodded to the donkey who was now silently watching me, and headed off feeling more in tune with the hills after having slept in a simple refuge.

The day's journey was a nightmare of climbing and descending over rocky paths, but I was slightly humiliated, and I thought that I had encountered ultimate courage, when I saw a man approaching at a vigorous pace in the company of two dogs on leashes that fanned out in front of him. He didn't seem to acknowledge my presence as I stepped to one side of the rocky path, and as he passed I saw that his head was held up, and although it was casting from side to side, his eyes were not following anything. I realised then that he had two guide dogs, and that he was completely blind. He was *hearing* the way along the GR10 by listening to the footfalls and motion of the dogs. I watched him disappear down the rocky trail expecting to see him go headlong at any second. He never seemed to falter or miss a step, and I continued up the path shaking my head. *Quelle courage* I thought.

Now, I'm cursed with an instinct for unintentional mimicry and imitation, and I now found myself walking the path to a count of ten or more, with my eyes shut, to find out what the blind man was experiencing. Naturally, I didn't consider that the absence of the two guide dogs would make any difference. Well they do, or would have, as a face-on collision with a silver birch taught me a little while later. Picking bits of papery bark from my nose with one hand, I gave it a taste of a walking pole with the other.

I later passed below the impressive ridge known as Larrun or La Rhune, and was just in time to see a train descending. I briefly considered running for it and getting transport out – but then how would I explain such cowardice? My photograph of the train, track angle, and trees shows exactly where I was on the trail at that moment – exactly at Les Trois Fontaines, and a stone's throw from one of the railway halts where it crosses the GR10. Such accurate positioning is not normally so simple or precise, and when it matters it's very welcome – as I was to find out on the first of June in dire circumstances.

Vultures were a very common sight during this part of the trail, and I became concerned during several of my rest breaks that they were a bit quick off the mark to circle over *me*! I didn't feel as bad as all that, and I would often make a few movements to let them know I wasn't ready for the plate yet. I once counted twenty three in one formation.

At one place, where I was passing below a steep cliff that looked as though it would be an ideal vulture roost, I paused to look up at this towering wall of rock. I'm still not certain of exactly what happened next, but as I craned my neck and head backwards to look up to the top, it seemed as though the sky was reeling. The next second I received a sharp slap on the back, and I thought something in the rucksack was trying to escape. It seemed like minutes, but I guess after only a couple of seconds I realised that I was now looking straight at the sky, and that the path had moved through ninety degrees and was now behind me. Raising my head to look, it seemed as though it was stretching out on each side from my feet. Could I have fallen into a black hole or been attacked by a vulture?

I had in fact, without any movement to save myself, simply toppled over backwards – rigid like a telegraph pole – presumably becoming unbalanced by looking up at the sky from the uneven ground.

I now lay in the heather, just off the track, like a sacrifice; slightly head-down and perfectly still, staring up at the sky. If there had been any onlookers it would have been quite a worthwhile spectacle, but unfortunately there were no witnesses and the unintentional performance was wasted.

In Sare, after encountering a few spots of rain though not enough to bring out the wet-wear, I again checked into a small hotel as compensation for the day's privations, but I bought provisions from an épicerie (grocer's) on the town square for a self-cooked meal.

Sitting cross-legged on the floor of the bathroom, I boiled six eggs on my gas stove, made soup, and also prepared a cold lunch of eggs, shallots and cheese for the following day. During this culinary diversion I looked up to see a man watching me from the window of a house on the opposite side of the street – he might at least have shouted *bon appétit!*

It was at Sare that I had an unfortunate encounter with an intruder in my room. This intruder was a cockroach, and I first became aware of it when I realised something was scuttling along the base of the skirting boards as I caught a movement on the edge of my vision. I gave chase immediately, because the image of it climbing the bedclothes during the night threatened to deprive me of sleep. The roach was too fast though for my first attempt to snare it with a wastepaper basket, and it made for the bathroom where I'm sure it had all sorts of safe houses prepared. I made one futile attempt to trap it in a tooth mug, but it retreated behind some pipes and seemed to watch me.

I then retreated a little way and watched it. We had a stalemate situation. I'd by this time armed myself with a floor cloth that I thought would give me a better chance – quick brute force was the only way I reckoned I'd get it, not the mincing positioning of a tooth mug.

After what was probably an eternity for the cockroach, but only a brief wait for me, it made its move. I've no idea why it emerged, it was out of reach where it had lurked behind the pipes, but suddenly it rushed me, either to intimidate me, or as a final suicidal and heroic gesture. There may of course have been others that were watching from the many crevices and insect fastnesses that abound in old-fashioned bathrooms with uneven wooden floors and exposed pipes. There may have been a spouse and little beetles perhaps, and this could have been, for the cockroach, a martyr's moment, a chance of immortality. Well, I made a swift defensive lurch with the cloth and squashed it horribly. The foul black mess of a squashed cockroach is something to be avoided at all costs, I was almost sick at the combination of the sight and sounds.

Sleep was difficult that night because of noisy clocks throughout the town, and I was haunted by visions of spiralling vultures, moving slowly in time to the Andy Pandy / Looby Loo theme.

Pays Basque Ouest, Pyrénées-Atlantiques

Day 4: Sare to Ainhoa

08:45 – 14:30

My memories of Sare faded fast. The room had been expensive, the bed / mattress had slanted to one side tending to roll me out, and I had some difficulty finding the exit trail from town (again). That was probably my lack of attention.

I saw a collie dog (a lassie type) about two kilometres outside Sare, and we walked together silently for awhile before he left me at a bend in the track just before a small bridge over a stream. It was about five kilometres later that I saw the same dog (I swear it was the same dog) coming proudly towards me. I assumed that at our first encounter it had been his intention to show me the shortest way, but that the GR10 had taken a detour. Again he just sort of hung around with me without being overtly attentive as I walked through a picnic area that could be reached from a nearby road. This was one of the more pleasant doggy companionships that was repeated occasionally during the following weeks – as was the phenomenon of the *GR10 Detour*.

I took a photograph of the collie, but as I took it he cocked his leg against a tree as a sort of comment I suppose, and I had a flashback to the dog peeing on the child's sandcastle at Brean. It was between sightings of the dog that I went knee-deep into a bog – not too pleasant, and I looked around to see if anyone had witnessed this literal *faux pas*.

After leaving the kind collie I was *properly* attacked, for the first time and not for the last time during the expedition, by an evil looking farm dog. It was determined to get a real bite and I had to constantly watch the animal as it ran round me in a circle trying to get inside the defences. The *Leki* walking poles proved a superb defence against this sort of hostility, and the sharp end was a good canine deterrent. These poles are absolutely indispensable for such defence and also for support on muddy tracks and passages. Steep ascents and descents are also much safer.

On this stage the route was often in narrow, low, leafy passageways running with water. It also passed through vast expanses of ancient woodland where I saw no sign of human life. Near the odd hamlet there might be an aged smallholder or gardener, but this was quite rare, and there was the first suggestion of remoteness.

At a relatively high place amidst some deserted Basque-style dwellings I relished the three surviving hard-boiled eggs and a baton of stale baguette.

I rolled into Ainhoa fairly tired but feeling ready for a beer which I took at the first bar. It is a satisfying experience to walk in without dragging the feet, or gasping red-faced and near death. I'm not kidding myself that this will not happen again though.

The first beer of the day at the bar set me up well enough to look for accommodation, but on finding out that it was another mile or so to a campsite, and in the opposite direction to the next day's route, I again took a hotel.

As I sat outside the splendid and cheap Hôtel Ohantzea with a beer, three off-road vehicles thundered past dramatically. They were full of passengers and bore adverts for *Excursions Pyrénéa*. It was at this point that trekker snobbery raised its head, and I snorted at those mechanised cheats.

I'd actually got into one or two walking rhythms today in all modes – up, down, and on the flat, and, although I was still totally knackered after only six hours and had yet again only completed a very short stage, I felt at ease with my beer.

The Hôtel Ohantzea was another oasis – really welcoming people. It was cosy, lots of very historic artefacts everywhere, and a quiet room with a small balcony at the rear of the hotel overlooking a secluded garden. Just right for stringing up smalls and a shirt to dry. I didn't realise it at the time but the room faced the following day's exit trail.

This hotel is well worth a visit, and in fact I revisited it by car with Lesley later in the year – the hospitality and sense of well-being was repeated, and the hotel owner remembered me from the walk which was warming.

Evening meal – Salade de gésiers (salad of duck's gizzards – one of my favourites), omelette aux cêpes (mushroom omelette), and a petit pichet de vin rouge (small carafe of red wine). The delightful landlady told me the hotel dated back to King Louis Quatorze, Louis XIV who lost his head during *la Terreur* – the terror which followed the French Revolution of

1789, and the sense of history and sense of place were quite palpable. On arrival I'd asked about cleaning my boots outside and she had said they didn't mind muddy boots at all – Rob at the Queen's Arms take note!

It's grey and rainy outside – hope it clears for tomorrow. The landlady says it's a hard route to Bidarray, so I hope the Ferme Esteban is still in business, else I could be bivvying.

Funny how some small details stand out, but I noticed that the salt and pepper cellars worked admirably at this hotel (salt and pepper on dry bread with a little vin rouge is a great hors d'oeuvres). The wine was Spanish and very good, and gradually as the wine went down, I felt better about the next day in spite of its potential hardship, than I had about previous days. Although nowhere near fit, I sensed a minute improvement that was not diminished by the aches and stiffness.

At Ainhoa I discovered that a practical way to wash a shirt and underwear is to initially wear them in the bath or shower, and then remove them to be rinsed after the body wash. There was a good long bath at Hôtel Ohantzea far better than the hip-bath at Sare.

I think I'll have the petit déjeuner here – I didn't have it at Sare. I also suspect that tea is best for me first thing – I'd tried coffee and chocolate first thing, but found that they made me thirsty later.

Day 5: Ainhoa to Bidarray
08:20 – 18:45

I was woken by a cockerel this morning, and by the sound of it, I should say that it was possibly *the* French national bird – It was so loud and persistent that it could have woken the Unknown Warrior atop l'Arc de Triomphe de l'Étoile in Paris as well as me. I wondered at first if it had got in the room overnight and gone under the bed it was so loud. Taking a quick peek – I would have caught it later anyway when I do my last-minute room inspection to make sure I've left nothing behind – I saw there was nothing noisier than an old sock and what looked like the stale middle section of a baguette. I checked my watch and saw that the time was 05:30. I had set the alarm for 06:30 and I then lay there in a wretched state of morning anxiety, waiting for it to go off. This was a big mistake, and I resolved <u>never</u> to set it again unless it was unavoidable. Cockerel permitting, I might have had another two hours peace before breakfast.

An early red sky was quickly replaced by grey and blue, with mists rolling over the mountains. Simple petit déjeuner and off onto the trail.

The walking route out of Ainhoa was on simple well-surfaced tracks and roads, though sometimes steep. The track then went up past the stations of the cross that lined the road for annual religious festivals. I carried on past the Chapel Ama Birjina where I stopped briefly and tried some of the only spring water that I'd seen so far. This issued from a pipe sticking out of the bank below the Madonna. With that pedigree it ought to be perfectly good – it was.

I arrived at the Chapelle de l'Aubépine at 390 metres and near the Calvary crucifixes – a group of large white crosses – in good time, and I paused here to admire the view back down the hill and to the stations of the cross that I had passed earlier. Those religious symbols were the basis for ceremonial processions up the hill to where I now stood in the shade.

It was while I was standing in this cool shade in a most unceremonious pose that I barely nodded to a walker who fairly shot past. I then saw an elderly lady following him at about a hundred metres and at a slower pace. I reckoned she was about sixty-five and I set out just as she arrived thinking that she would probably rest at the chapel. She asked me in French if the chapel was open and I replied that I didn't know, and carried on up the hill. As I was struggling up the continuing gradient I realised that this lady was keeping pace with me. Further on, desperate for one of my frequent rests, I realised with horror that she was actually gaining on me. Eventually I stopped and tried to look French to save mine and the nation's honour, hoping that she would keep going. I'd very nearly collapsed, and I was the colour of a British postbox from my efforts to out-distance her.

No such luck.

She strode purposefully at me rather than towards me, stopped within striking distance and said with a twinkle in her eye, "Français?"

At this point I realised the game was up and I replied defiantly, "Anglais!"

"I thought so," she said, and went on to tell me that she was from Stroud in Gloucestershire. She informed me that the man in front was Klaus, a German, and somewhat younger than me. It turned out that Molly was sixty-nine and a lifelong mountain walker with her husband Norman who could no longer roam the hills because of angina. Molly was good company at this stage, and we set off at a continuous pace that was fine but which I would probably not have made if I'd been left to my own lazy wanderings.

We caught Klaus at Ferme Esteban where he was tucking into the plat du jour – omelette et jambon. Well we didn't exactly catch him, that makes it sound as though we snared or trapped him. He was a good fellow, and I was to walk with him for quite some distance over several days. Molly ate at Ferme Esteban as well, but I decided to eat some of my rucksack – I regarded it as a single malevolent entity by this stage. It, and everything in it, possessed the characteristics of something like a flock of birds, in a relationship of corporate empathy. Any individual part had an identity, but they could all combine to form one belligerent and maybe objectionable whole. So I ate some of it – made it lighter – that'll teach it I thought.

Molly was telling me about her walking interests and her family in considerable detail while we walked. To try and answer her every time would have been more exhausting than walking so I found I could just grunt an acknowledgement now and again and get away with it. I later walked with another man in his sixties, and he could also talk for hours while walking. I couldn't do it, and I wondered whether they had extra gills, or hollow bones like birds maybe?

When I left Ainhoa I'd planned to stay at Ferme Esteban, but having made good time pacing Molly I decided to go on to Bidarray with them. It had been in my mind anyway to go that whole distance as a trial run at such a daily stage. Especially since I'd already divided Castle's single stage between Olhette and Ferme Esteban into three!

Not unexpectedly, Klaus quickly disappeared over the horizon before we were half a kilometre outside Ferme Esteban, leaving Molly and I to walk together. This was fine, and I learned from Molly that on steep ascents she paced herself at about one mile per hour. This was the first time I had considered the principle of consciously regulating and monitoring the pace. I'd always found myself careering along at all sorts of paces on all sorts of slopes, with the marching songs generally fitting in with whatever I could manage. This was partly what was knackering me – no discipline. Story of my life I thought. This realisation was to prove a watershed and, a few days later, it would give my teeth a new lease of life.

Past the Col des Veaux at 540 metres, along the Spanish border, and a climb up to the Col Méhatche; and then onto the road for awhile. Shortly after this there was a horrendous descent for about three kilometres down a cliff face, over scree, and along a twelve inch wide goat track with a ravine about two hundred metres deep on one side – this was serious stuff.

We eventually arrived at the gîte d'étape at Bidarray only to find it closed – contrary to published information. The final approach had been up a road that was so steep that I found it pleasant to walk backwards for a while. Mustn't do that too often I thought. Some anxious enquiries revealed that as a last resort there was a hotel nearby, but that a warden should be available a little later to open the gîte. Molly contemplated the hotel and a bar meal, while I slunk around the town, just managing to buy some victuals before the small and only village shop closed. I had a Coke and watched some energetic youngsters playing football.

I made my own pea and ham soup, ate two cartons of yoghurt, and then ate some bread that Molly didn't eat with her bar meal of omelette and chips – very popular and common everywhere – and finished up with a couple of pur beurre (rich butter) biscuits. Appetite can be a strange thing, and it was not the only occasion on which I just didn't fancy anything else.

When we eventually identified the warden, and Molly decided that the gîte was preferable to the hotel, we turned out to be the only occupants of the gîte – except for the mosquitoes – although a very large party of school-aged walkers was arriving next day. There were several pallets of packed lunches laid out invitingly, and I was sorely tempted. I'm sure they wouldn't have missed just one pack.

I slept very badly, and woke the next morning with a stiff back, and barely able to move. Brufen to the rescue. It turned out that Klaus had not found the warden, and had stayed at the hotel – if we had known, then Molly and I might have joined him for a beer at least.

Day 6: Bidarray to Saint-Étienne-de-Baïgorry
09:00 – 20:00

On the way to Saint-Étienne I parted from Molly at a point where she could take a shortcut to a small village called Urdos since it was 15:00, and the remaining journey to Saint-Étienne could be several hours. I had a bivvy-bag and sleeping bag and was able to sleep rough if necessary, whereas she needed hotel accommodation. My friend Terry phoned me just at that junction by chance. The biggest surprise was that there was a signal at all.

The rest of the day was my first full-stage walk without company. I'd walked alone during the preceding days, but the terrain was now getting more serious. There were many lonely stretches across ridges, through woods and up and down scree slopes. The only other signs of life were some wild goats, as big as donkeys, that looked disapprovingly from their mountain retreats. I was beginning to enjoy the day and had stopped in a wood to complete the inevitable water cycle – i.e. in through the mouth, predominantly out through the skin, but always completed with that last satisfying relief when taken in the open air behind a tree.

Anyway, I'd looked around as usual to ensure privacy, I'd whistled and made some appropriate sounds of satisfaction, and I'd issued a few curses when the Leki poles refused to stay where they were put and attempted an escape back down the hill. I was just smiling contentedly when I caught a movement among some rocks about forty feet away and slightly above and off the track to the left. Almost soundlessly, a hill walker – clearly Basque – made his way back to the track, where I was pretending to have just stopped to admire the forest.

This man of the woods was a very pleasant young fellow, clad in simple natural material walking clothing with a simple wooden staff, he had piercing eyes and a manner that was totally at ease with the rich austerity of the countryside. I'd been totally unaware of his presence, and he must have smiled, watching me bumbling around in my ignorance. We chatted briefly about the magnificence of the mountains, about rugby, and about his trip from Bayonne for a day's walking. I was to meet several people during the next few weeks who were just simply a part of the scenery, not an imposition like I felt. They were natural hill folk, unsophisticated but completely in control of their relationship with nature.

Further on I startled some goats who ran away in front of me, round and up the gradient to the right, and then back behind me to regain their preferred bit of scrubby pasture. As they passed above me they caused a small cascade of stones, and some larger rocks the size of a football that bounced over the track just missing me. I made a mental note to watch out for this sort of hazard in future.

One sort of hazard, which seemed so unpredictable and persistent that there was no defence against it, was caused by the pole-grabbers in the heather. I encountered these mischievous miscreants on many occasions, and later in the adventure, one even succeeded in making off with the flange from the base of my daughter's Leki pole. We searched in vain at that time for the flange and the culprit, but the heather had closed ranks over the incident, and we were denied a conviction.

Walking with poles mostly involves an alternating motion as the arms naturally swing backwards and forwards as they do when walking along a road for instance. One pole trails *momentarily,* and can be used to push, while the other is advanced. More rarely, on steep downhill stretches for example, both poles might be placed in front together to act as a brake. The unseen threat in question would wait until the natural walking motion took me past the trailing pole, and just as the dynamic balance called for this pole to be brought smartly forward, I would find that it had been seized, and was firmly anchored in the grip of something that I imagined to be about the size of a rabbit, but with the muscles and outlook of an adolescent badger that had been reared on anabolic steroids. The grip, no doubt reinforced by more than one of these beasts, was sometimes enough to spin me sideways, and more than once I was nearly yanked off my feet. The creatures were always gone by the time I'd regained my balance and thrown myself at the area around the base of the pole. I assumed they were scuttling on to the next suitable ambush position.

After a few of these unwarranted attacks, I was so angry, that on one occasion, as I felt that first tug, I let go the pole, whirled round, and jumped into the heather to cut it off. Cursing loudly, I thrashed several square metres with the free pole, but naturally there was nothing there.

After one particularly bad incident with a pole-grabber, it was during the negotiation of a particularly challenging rocky stretch that I was enlightened about the annoying toothache I'd been experiencing. It was, in fact, more of a complete face-ache. As I picked my way through a stony part of the path, one of the marching songs was going through my mind with the volume turned to maximum. It was deafening, and I was keeping time with my feet, and mentally going over the words. It was the Gay Gordons tune, and I was just reaching the point where the canary emerges, gasping, from Auntie Mary's drawers. I was expecting the applause to start at any second.

Possibly because of heightened awareness brought on by the pole-grabbers' persistence I became aware of a drumming and clacking sound that seemed to surround me. I stopped and it stopped. I suddenly realised that it had been with me since the start of the more strenuous walking that commenced as I left Hendaye. I started forwards again, and as the applause for the canary began, the clacking and grinding was there again.

This sudden realisation that it was my own teeth which were crashing and grinding in time with the walking and to the wild symphonic accompaniment was a traumatic shock of the first order. This was no relaxing holiday, this was a forced march in captivity. I took off the rucksack and sat down to consider what was to be done about it.

After some thought I came to the conclusion that I wouldn't be able to stop the marching songs but I just might be able to prevent a large dentist's bill when I got home; and it would also be good to avoid premature dentures. I rejected the idea of stuffing a handkerchief in my mouth because the image of me walking through the hills like that was just not on – I had some pride – and anyway I didn't have a clean enough handkerchief. I'd just have to listen out for it, and hope I could control it.

The grinding and clacking did diminish somewhat after this understanding, and within a day or so I thought I had it conquered.

The day's journey eventually terminated in Saint-Étienne-de-Baïgorry, just opposite the Hôtel Izzara which was too tempting to resist.

I was as usual totally knackered. I had a small beer, garbure, jambon de Bayonne, blanquette d'Agneau with six chips in their jackets, crème brulée the size of a soup plate, and a small pichet of vin rouge. I didn't finish the chips, wine or crème brulée. I must have been bad.

Over a beer I chatted with Claude, the easy-going, open-natured barman about rugby, Leicester having just beaten one of their local teams that day towards the end of the game. I attempted to have a conversation with another elderly local, but after struggling for about five or ten minutes we were clearly getting nowhere – he seemed to be speaking some strange French or Basque dialect that was unintelligible. The barman, smiling, later told me the elderly chap was Bosnian.

Back still bad, more Brufen.

Day 7: Saint-Étienne-de-Baïgorry to Saint-Jean-Pied-de-Port
09:00 – 18:30

On the way out of town I paused to watch a game of Pelota one of the characteristic Basque games, typically played on a Sunday morning at the town *Fronton* – a high wall. I was also lucky enough to find an open Pharmacie (Chemist's shop) where I could get some citron-flavoured energy tablets.

On the initial ascent out of Saint-Étienne-de-Baïgorry I decided to try my first, non iodine-treated spring water, and I chose a site where water was dripping over stones just above the road. The important thing is to try and ensure that there is no habitation, or dead animal above the point where the water is taken. The approach looked clear, so I sniffed and tried the waters. Other than a slight grittiness it was fine. I would now have to wait and see if there was going to be any Pyrénéan revenge.

Today was much cooler, and grey – good for walking – and a few miles before Saint-Jean-Pied-de-Port, on Mont Manhoa at 1021 metres, I stopped for sardines, stale bread, and two handfuls of raisins. Glancing at my watch, and remembering it was Sunday, I wistfully realised my friends would all be in the Queen's Arms at home. Another idle glance at the mobile phone showed one of those rare moments when there was a usable signal, and I knew what I had to do. Although everyone knew I'd set off on this trip, they refused to believe that I was on a mountain-top in the Pyrénées, and suggested that I was in hiding somewhere in the U.K., and just waiting until enough time had elapsed to allow me to return. After the brief chat, I looked around at the approaching mist and again wondered, not for the last time, what on earth I was doing this for.

Looking to the distant Northeast towards Saint-Jean-Pied-de-Port, I could see very little because of mist, just a purple haze, and the gentle uplift beyond, but over to the left, the nearer slopes of the Irouléguy wine producing region were clearly visible. My memories of Irouléguy from a few years previous, were not too complementary, but I resolved to investigate the development of this little known wine.

It was cold enough to require my coat on the final descent to the plain that leads to Saint-Jean-Pied-de-Port, and the warmer lower level was welcome. Dog attacks again, however, on passing through a small village called appropriately, Lasse, were not so welcome. By this time, after almost being nipped earlier, I had a technique. Show no fear, and at the slightest provocation – a small growl will do – go for the dog first. I later had the satisfaction of terrifying a couple of small, hairy, fairly quiescent genetic excuses for dogs. At Lasse though, a huge farm dog threateningly shot out at me from a gateway on the right of the track; but, before I could make a lunge with a Leki pole, it unexpectedly veered away to one side, and, snarling horribly, deliberately crashed and stamped in a patch of undergrowth while seeming to ignore me – at least it was avoiding eye contact. I was reminded of the behaviour of Gorillas that will make a show of strength and destruction before committing to an actual physical encounter.

Fortunately, there were no witnesses of the ridiculous exchange that followed – the dog barked and stamped without looking at me, and I shouted and waved my poles in the air without looking at the dog. We both eventually left the field with honour, and, looking back over my shoulder, I saw just the dog's head above the long grass as it silently watched me leave its territory. The farms of the Basque country were the worst area for this type of behaviour, and also for the more direct biting attempts.

The final approach to Saint-Jean-Pied-de-Port was a dreary road walk past garages, and drab, little-used buildings outside the old city walls.

I snapped up the first candidate once inside these old city walls – the Hôtel des Ramparts. Two nights demi-pension and a rest day tomorrow – hooray. Today's short and easy stage was still very tiring. I know I have to lighten the rucksack or I won't finish the whole trail. The compensation of the day was again, of course, the dinner of the day – piperade omelette (tomato and onion), duck and chips with green salad, followed by tartelette aux pommes. No Gâteau Basque unfortunately – maybe tomorrow I was told.

Once again my request for vinegar with the chips was greeted with a quizzical look and raised eyebrows as if I was mad; and this time it came in a glass bowl with what I decided was a runcible spoon.

Flies in restaurants and hotels at this time of year can be a real problem. In this one they were buzzing the food and, since I had very short, cropped hair, I could feel them doing circuits of landing and taking off from the inviting plateau of the top of my head. I discussed the phenomenon with la patronne, and she told me that it was worse this year than ever before.

A diner across the room had the solution. He had a fat cigar in one hand that he kept glowing to maintain a wreath of smoke round his and his companion's heads while he ate his food between puffs. I was glad of the distance between us, but resented being forced to entertain his share of the flies.

I think he was Belgian.

Day 8: Rest at Saint-Jean-Pied-de-Port

A relaxing sunny market day was an ideal break from walking. Any day would be an ideal break from walking, and I took the chance to send some items back home by post in order to lighten the load.

My Buffalo shirt, lightweight / shower-proof jacket, gas burner, binoculars, spare tent pegs, Bill Bryson's book (now completed), and the huge manual that came with my multi-function altimeter / watch all took a trip home. I later also left a gas canister, flares, and a leather belt in a spare zip-up container with the patronne of the Hôtel des Ramparts, with the assurance that I would return in a month or two by car to collect them – if I survived the remaining trek. The flares had been thoughtfully included as a dual purpose safety and bear defence aid. I subsequently realised that they would have been of little use in either event

The market as usual was mainly clothes and cheap footwear, but there were one or two attractive food and drinks stalls. It was torment to be unable to buy large quantities of these delights because I had no car, and I couldn't afford to take on more weight. Instead, I satisfied myself tasting a range of saucisson – wild boar, horse, pork, beef, and, surprisingly – donkey! They all tasted more or less the same, spicy and smoky.

I did find two bandanas, one of which bore the words *Pays Basque* together with the Basque emblem. I decided that one could go round my neck, and the larger plain one would fit my head. Although I never used the head version – it seemed a bit over-the-top at my age – I was never without the neckerchief, and I felt proud to wear it. I still use it at times to this day.

I located the Porte d'Espagne that I mistakenly thought at this time was the GR10 continuation, failed to find a Pharmacie to buy some more flavouring for water, and discussed the travel characteristics of different types of saucisson with a charcutier (pork butcher). The best type for unrefrigerated transport has the lowest fat content and should be quite dry. I reserved a fine, dry specimen to be collected early the next day, along with some bread from the boulangerie next door – and I just narrowly escaped buying a delicious-looking spit-roasted, corn-fed chicken that was one of a small flock that beckoned to me from a rotisserie outside. It wouldn't have travelled well I told myself, and I was trying hard to restrict my food intake. But the heavenly aroma – it was irresistible, and I found myself turning and being drawn towards them like steel to a magnet.

It was only by the greatest effort and with a pathetic whimper that I managed to break the spell and continue miserably on my way with an occasional backwards glance at the beauties.

Having thus achieved the tasks that I'd set for the day, I left the market and the usual group of beggars with brand new designer trainers and dogs to support, and made for a suitable hostelry that I'd noted earlier. Before I left, one particular dog eyed me suspiciously as I caught its eye. I looked sideways at it, and without anyone else noticing, just vaguely pointed a Leki pole in its direction. It fidgeted without a sound and looked away – I reckoned word had got round, don't tangle with the baton Anglais.

Since I'd committed to the evening meal at the hotel, I fully intended to just have a glass of Irouléguy at a bar on the central traffic roundabout in town. This might sound like a busy interchange, but it's a fine spot to watch life go by. It's right on the junction between the GR10 and the GR65 pilgrimage route from Le Puy in the Auvergne, to Santiago de Compostela in northwest Spain, and although I didn't spot any obvious pilgrims there was a real spirit of place.

Well, after the one glass – I had to admit that those wine glasses are sometimes a bit on the small side – and at 14:15, the barman's trap sprang shut and I was snared again. A moderately sized salade campagnarde (country salad) of gésiers (duck gizzards again) and lardons (streaky bacon pieces), with which I'm quite familiar, was excellently enhanced by the addition of walnuts and Iraty d'Ossau cheese – the latter sheep's milk cheese being reputedly the oldest type of cheese in the world.

Washed down with some more magnificently chewy Irouléguy, the snack was memorable and all the more enjoyable because of its chance occurrence. I really didn't mean to have it, I tried hard not to have it, but I'm afraid I've no will power when it comes to avoiding food. On the way back to the hotel, I again passed the rotisserie with its last one or two, now dejected and crest-fallen, inmates. No temptation this time. Well, only a little.

Contemplating after the meal – some of my best ideas seem to come after a meal or in the bath – I decided to try a citron teabag in my belt flask of cold water. This belt flask is a half litre container that I use on-the-fly for drinking, and which I then top up as necessary from the two litre container that I keep at the centre of the corporate rucksack. I position it so that it's easy to pull out without unpacking everything and, being inside the sack, the main supply stays cool and makes me stop to get it each time I get through a half litre. That way I'm obliged to take a rest whether I want one or not – I don't need much excuse – and I then know how much I've got in reserve in the sack.

The citron teabags turned out to be a very good way of taking the mustiness out of some of the water sources – the teabags are very light to carry and the albeit small amount of caffeine is always welcome.

The evening meal was slightly marred by the fact that the floor of the restaurant had just been cleaned, and the whole dining room smelled of disinfectant. This only gradually faded, although I think it was more a case of getting used to the smell. Nevertheless, the conventional hors d'oeuvres, côte de porc, and a superb Gâteau Basque were an excellent end to the Saint-Jean experience.

After the meal I strolled around the town as the sun left a clear, darkening blue sky, and my final thoughts of the day were that this area was still really only the foothills – what would the real thing be like?

Day 9: Saint-Jean-Pied-de-Port to Estérençuby
08:00 – 15:00

This variant stage of the GR10 was a fairly uneventful day, much of it on roads and well-marked tracks, the exit from Saint-Jean being to the east of the town and not via the Port d'Espagne to the southwest.

About half an hour into the trek I got a very welcome and encouraging *Bon Courage* from an elderly gentleman who was sitting by a fountain in the central square of a small village named Caro about four miles southeast from Saint-Jean-Pied-de-Port. I returned the salute with a cheery wave of a walking pole.

It was very blue and sunny, roasting and sweaty; so it was with dismay that I arrived at Estérençuby to find that the gîte d'étape was fully booked due to some motorcycle event in the neighbourhood. Where that was, was difficult to understand since we were pretty remote, and there did not seem to be any populated neighbourhood. The gîte was administered by the hotel next door – Hôtel Andreinia. Above the door was a sign announcing that it was the domain of *Le Patron Larramendy*. It seemed a bit pretentious, but this turned out to be the only accommodation. There was some sort of government refuge nearby, but they wouldn't let me in.

I was shown to a room and I decided to take a rest for about an hour before the usual bar and dining routine. After about fifteen minutes however, I found that I'd developed a headache, and that there was a strong electrical type of humming noise in the room. As I moved about the room, I realised that the intensity varied, and that it seemed most intense right where the pillow lay on the bed. I never found an explanation for this, and the patron offered no resistance when I told him the room was unacceptable because it seemed as though I had a large invisible insect as a room mate. I was shown to a new room, and had wonderful silence except for the soporific sound of the river outside.

Rested, showered, and generally spruced up, I decided that the bar and restaurant just had to be visited. The walls were decorated with photographs of local hunters, and a large painted cartoon of two hunters being chased by a wild boar and a rabbit. On closer inspection I realised that one of the photographs had been taken in front of the hotel, and showed four or five cars with hunters kneeling in front and presenting their weapons, like a scene from the film *The Deer Hunter*. Strapped to the bonnet of each car, legs hanging down each side of the car, was the biggest and ugliest collection of *sangliers* – wild boar – imaginable. These beasts were huge.

When I engaged the barman, André, in conversation, he told me that the hills around the area were full of them. I was quiet for awhile, and wondered whether sangliers had ever encountered chilli powder before. I had a horrible suspicion that they might be beyond such trivial irritants. I asked him if they had yet developed a taste for human or tourist flesh. The barman and one or two locals laughed at this, and, hey presto, we had a rapport for an evening's jest and amusement I thought.

I'd broadened the topic to the general safety of wild camping in the area, and had drawn in a glassy-eyed fellow who was already, judging by his bloodshot eyes and drooping posture, on his second bottle of Ricard. On the subject of perils in the woods, he put his hand out horizontally, and waggled it.

"Ça va – maintenant," he said mysteriously, avoiding eye contact.

The action with the hands, the pause after the *Ça va*, and the emphasis in the voice on the word *maintenant* – i.e. now – implied one of two things. Either that it wasn't safe before, but that it *might* be now; or, that it was now, but that it *might not* be tomorrow. Either way, the future was going to be interesting in respect of wild beasts.

He shook his head, knocked back another Ricard, and wouldn't be drawn further. I was just on the point of loosening his tongue with another Ricard, when Molly entered the bar, and all conversation and talk centred on her.

Shortly afterwards Klaus walked in after having lost his way among the variants of the GR10 and GR65, and after having bull-dozed his way across country to arrive here partly by chance. He looked like a hairy tomato coated in condensation.

After returning home, I later found that this happened to him again in more testing circumstances, not far from where I almost came to grief on the Hourquette d'Arre. But that's later in this tale.

When Molly and Klaus were settled in and the inevitable excitement when news arrives had died down, I managed to get a word again with Monsieur *Ricard* who had consumed another bottle at the bar. I showed him my guidebook by Alan Castle, *The Pyrénéan Trail GR10*, and flicking through the pages he stopped at a picture of Mont Vignemale – an awe-inspiring sight, and a mountain which was first climbed by a French couple, Henri Cazaux and Bernard Guillembet in 1837. Vignemale was later made famous when the Irish-French Count Henry Russell purchased a ninety-nine year lease of the mountain from the town hall of Cauterets in 1889. For this awesome piece of real-estate, he paid the princely sum of one Franc per year! As my bar companion sat staring at the photograph, his eyes went even more glassy and moist, and he seemed far away in some reverie.

"C'est formidable, eh!" I whispered, hating to break the spell, to which he made no reply other than holding up a thumb, and staring into his Ricard – one of many more.

Molly saved me from any more of this pathetic example of sentiment, by getting me to call her a taxi for the next day from the payphone outside. She wanted to be sure of getting to Lescun, and we were told that the motorcycle crowds had taken all places in several of the gîtes d'étape further along the trail. I wasn't sure that a taxi ride really counted along the GR10, but then a lot of people walked various stages without feeling obliged to do the whole thing on foot, or to walk all the way.

I'd found today that I was still tiring easily on uphill stretches, but that downhill was not as bad as previously. It was encouraging, and once more I knew that I would have to walk all the way.

After a meal taken with Molly and Klaus, of garbure, omelette jambon, and a simple apple, I slept well that night with the windows open, deep lungfuls of fresh air, and a good musical river. As far as I remember my sleep was untroubled by nightmares of wild boar or any other perils of wild camping.

Selected Photographs Pays Basque Ouest

Day 01 – 14 May 08:55
The rucksack posing by the first ballise in Hendaye.

Day 02 – 15 May 17:15
The view looking back towards the Atlantic from just before Col d'Ibardin. Col d'Osin is in the distance, right of centre.

Day 03 – 16 May 13:06
A tempting chance to run for the train below La Rhune.

Day 03 – 16 May 14:07
Vultures on the way to Sare.

Day 04 – 17 May 09:22
Sharing the GR10 with a stream in a woodland tunnel towards Ainhoa.

Day 04 – 17 May 12:03
A typical deserted house on the troubled frontier.

Day 05 – 18 May 09:22
Looking back at the Stations Of The Cross on the way to La Chapelle de l'Aubépine.

Day 06 – 19 May 16:43
Just before the descent to Saint-Étienne-de-Baïgorry.

Day 07 – 20 May 14:59
Mont Manhoa at 1021 metres, approaching Saint-Jean-Pied-de-Port.

Day 08 – 21 May 14:15
Chewing a glass of delicious Irouléguy at a bar on the central traffic roundabout.

Day 09 – 22 May 14:56
Entering Estérençuby.

4   Pays Basque Est, Pyrénées-Atlantiques
Day 10: Estérençuby to Chalet Pedro
08:15 – 16:00

After breakfast Molly took her taxi, Klaus disappeared into the distance, and I set off at my own pace into the grey, misty, cloudy, clammy, sweaty stage. I made a good steady climb up the road, and ascended about 200 metres at a rate of just faster than one pace a second without any break. Six hundred feet or so up without stopping – I thought I'd cracked it. The secret is to find your own pace and not attempt to match anyone else; and don't let yourself go, even when alone, at a pace that cannot be maintained. Obvious to any experienced walker I suppose, and with hindsight, obvious to anyone – other than me. These pearls of wisdom were beginning to coalesce after my talks and walks with Molly.

This was great, and in this frame of mind, about three kilometres short of the Sommet d'Occabé, I left the route without realising it. I didn't look at the compass when I took a right turn that I *assumed* was correct, and I didn't notice what I later saw was a very clear X sign which indicated that this was NOT the GR10. I was very lucky, because less than half a kilometre down the wrong track I met a berger (shepherd) and stopped for a brief chat about the weather. I asked if it was going to be sunny, and he said that it ought to be – *il faudra* – I think. Off the cuff I nodded down the track and said, not really inviting any denial, "Chalet Pedro?" to which he said no, and pointed back up the track and to the right – "The GR10? No, the track's back there Monsieur," in heavily accented French.

I think my mouth fell open and I looked at him idiotically, and frankly disbelievingly. I made him repeat the correction, looked sufficiently humbled, and retraced my steps.

I'd been on the way south to Spain and, though I like to think that I would have realised that I'd missed the Sommet before too long, I could have lost hours and a lot of well-being.

Reaching the place where I'd gone wrong I saw the red negation sign clearly, and with the compass I found a *ballise* (white over red) in the correct direction. This was, unfortunately, seriously upwards across a grassy expanse which was littered with stones, dung, and some seriously challenged vegetation. It was terrible from that point on, and I wondered if I'd earlier sub-consciously made a better decision to go to Spain instead.

Mist, less than one hundred metres visibility, soaked to the skin, muggy, cold, clammy – all at the same time. I had to use the altimeter, compass, and pedometer for guidance, though the faithful *ballises* were always there when looked for.

I blessed the people who maintained those markers, and just two weeks later I would encounter one with a pot of white, and a pot of red paint, and would have the opportunity to thank him profusely for his efforts. That encounter was to be on Day 25 during the delightful floral approach to a village named Grust.

The Cromlech stones and the Sommet d'Occabé almost went unnoticed in the mist, but a slight lightening showed when I was there. I perched the poles on the small undulating plateau and wandered for a while among the albeit small relics of an ancient time. They were ghostly and mysterious in the mist, as all standing stones are, but these were far more atmospheric than most because of the location and the current weather. Totally isolated, and with the limited visibility, it was easy to imagine a family from the bronze age stepping into view. I wondered what would have been on the menu in such a remote and isolated place, and whether they would have had wine at this altitude.

After that there were many pleasant and silent pauses so that I could listen to the birdsong and absorb the peace as I dropped down through the woods towards Chalet Pedro. There were many old, moss-covered, fallen trees among the woods, and I remember well that the area seemed dark and mysterious, though not in any way threatening.

A few hundred metres out from Chalet Pedro the trees had thinned, although the high canopy of leaves was still unbroken, and there was visibility for many metres across smooth brown soil. The ground was completely devoid of any vegetation, but it was criss-crossed every so often by a tangle of tree roots that looked for all the world like thousands of snakes. I knew that adders were common in the Pyrénées, and I now realised why I hadn't seen any earlier. They were all here.

I was just contemplating this serpentine scene, and wondering how I could get past the winding obstacle without being bitten, when I saw Klaus walking back up the slope towards me. I just stifled a warning shout, and waited, treacherously, to see if he'd be overwhelmed. He didn't seem to see anything amiss, and told me he'd arrived earlier, but hadn't found any accommodation, and although there seemed to be a small group of chalets, they didn't open till July, even though a girl was present with her dog and was expecting someone else to arrive. It was all *a bit vague* Klaus told me. He'd walked back up the trail to see if I was about.

Klaus said he'd left his pack at the chalet, and when we got there we found that the girl's dog had eaten his scarf, hat, and map / guidebook. Well, it had very nearly eaten them; they were just about recognisable as evidence, and he was actually very lucky that the dog seemed to know which pages of his guide had already been covered, since most of the trail ahead was still identifiable with a bit of imagination.

The girl said that the dog was very naughty and that she was very sorry. Klaus said that he was very sorry as well, and that the hat was one of his favourites. I said nothing and tried to keep a straight face, while making a stealthy motion at the dog with a Leki pole to try and get it into further trouble. The dog though, was a young Labrador, disarmingly full of beans (along with Klaus's possessions), and it seemed totally at ease with the crime, and also immune to threats with the baton Anglais. The doggy grapevine obviously didn't reach this far. As the girl talked, the dog sat and looked enthusiastically, first at Klaus and then at me, as if waiting to see which one she was going to nominate as the next victim. It really was quite a charming and happy dog, I thought, but then it hadn't eaten any of my belongings.

The girl offered to drive to Saint-Jean-Pied-de-Port to find a replacement map book for Klaus, although she didn't offer to do anything specific about the hat and scarf, and Klaus defiantly wore these tatters frequently afterwards. I took Klaus to one side, and we discussed how the canine outrage could be turned to our advantage. I decided that Klaus needed a manager or at least a witness in this affair, and my cut would be a share of his compensation. This turned out well, and the girl agreed to open a couple of the chalets for us as long as we would be OK with any over-wintering mice that hadn't yet taken their summer break. She prepared confit de porc (pork preserved in fat) with cassoulet (another of my favourites), and an excellent Gâteau Basque. She furthermore presented Klaus with a bottle of wine to compensate for the damaged neckwear and headwear. I pointed out to Klaus, that to drink a whole bottle of wine would be imprudent and possibly dangerous in the mountains, so we shared that as well. I had of course seen him drink a bottle with barely a pause for breath, but we were partners in this after all.

It was, as the French say, *une bonne affaire* – a good deal – and we slept well to the sound of another musical river nearby.

Day 11: Chalet Pedro to Logibar

10:00 – 19:15

Klaus and I set off together, and in general I kept to his pace without trouble. From Col Bagarguiac we chose the long, older GR10 variant instead of the shorter route to Larrau. That would have been his idea of course. The day was hot and sunny with clear blue skies, and the route consisted of a lot of climbing and descending over rocky tracks in places. The route is not recommended in bad weather, and it occurred to me that I wouldn't recommend it in *any* weather.

As we approached the Crête Ugatzé at 1170 metres, I found that Klaus was pulling away from me, with his tattered, dog-eaten scarf blowing out behind him like a battle flag. Now, although I knew that this was unwise, I went against my own now-understood rules. I quickened my pace to keep up. We seemed to rocket past three walkers to whom I nodded and offered a breathless *bonjour* (I didn't catch any reply), and we hurtled along the track.

This was not my style of mountain-loafing at all, and, after about ten minutes, I mouthed some silent dismissal at Klaus and slowed down. I continued to slow down until I collapsed beneath a tree. I was just losing the facial beetroot tones, and breathing almost normally, when the three walkers came past at a pleasant relaxed pace. I waved a limp hand in greeting and they smiled and went past. The last in line, a bearded jovial fellow, looked at me and, smiling, said simply, "So!"

It sounded like *Zo!* which really implied, *a fat lot of good racing did you!*

I was reminded of the parable of the hare and the tortoise, although I was certainly no hare and they were not in the least tortoise-like. I felt I'd got the worst of both worlds, and resolved again to be a bit more disciplined. They turned out to be German-speaking Swiss, and a really good bunch. I regret that I did not make a note of their addresses. They recommended the GR20 in Corsica as one of the most taxing of the GR series.

I finally tipped up at the gîte d'étape at Logibar and saw from some distance beforehand that the umbrella-shaded bar area outside was fairly packed with people, the three Swiss among them, but no sign of Klaus. This was the first real encounter with more than just a couple or so of other walkers. The gîte was indeed full, and when I eventually found Klaus I was relieved to find that he'd booked me in. He'd arrived and had a shower while I smelled the flowers, watched the butterflies, and listened to the silence in the woods above Logibar.

At this point I should add that Klaus has done many Alpine treks and is younger than I am. Anyway, we went up to the three Swiss at their table as if we were old friends – camaraderie in the hills is instinctive – and I bought a round of beers. We joked about pacing, and two of the Swiss said that the other fellow, Martin, was notorious for racing off, and that they never tried to match his pace. I did indeed see proof of this a day or so later.

That evening, there were lots of us – all packed into a small, wood-panelled upstairs dining room. Everyone had eaten garbure (unfortunately, just potato soup really), steak and cube-shaped chips, crème caramel. There was a great atmosphere, but it was a shame about the food.

Inspecting the bedroom arrangements I found that I'd been allocated a shared, two-level, three per level bunk, and that the Swiss were my bed-fellows. There were about eight or ten of us in the room, and it was about fifteen feet square – god help us, I thought.

Some of the sleepers had turned in while it was still light, and were clearly asleep. Others were preparing for bed, and everyone was being very considerate. This early slumbering really was totally unfair, as I later realised that the first snorer to get to sleep had the best night. A Frenchman snored all night and got the prize for keeping the rest of us awake. I was awake until about 03:00. Klaus thought it was me that was snoring, and our friendship was in peril until I explained that it wasn't me it was the Frenchman, and that anyway, his (Klaus's) socks stank so badly that it was a wonder any of us were still alive. He accepted that his socks were a problem and grinned.

I was very tired the next day, and that was to be a very long challenging day.

Day 12: Logibar to Sainte-Engrâce
09:15 – 19:45

I don't know if the Swiss had tried to get into the small room at Logibar and had been put off by the snoring competition, but they seemed to have found an alternative sleeping area, and we didn't see them again until they arrived at Sainte-Engrâce after both of us.

The day was grey, misty, clammy, soaking wet, and sweaty. Klaus and I set off together from Logibar, and climbed the long path through trees, and later, over open ground, towards the Gorges d'Holzarté with the river on our right. We walked a lot of the way at the same pace. The suspension bridge known as the Passerelle d'Holzarté was built in 1922, and I hoped that it was still in good condition since it was several hundred feet to the river below. I was mildly surprised to recognise the Passerelle from a visit a few years earlier with my family and a group of friends. It had been August then, and the whole party, in spite of frantic bracken-waving, had been eaten alive at this tourist trap, by vile-looking large black horse-flies. I kept looking about me in case there were more this time, but guessed that in May they were still in hibernation. As it turned out, they had obviously all migrated to the desolate Ariège region, where they were preparing to welcome me later in June.

Some way further on, Klaus continued at his break-neck pace, and I fell into my dawdling, aimless pace that at least allowed me to see what was around me. That would have been more correct if it hadn't been so misty. The way markers were difficult to see in places – the white and red *ballises* just discernible at about 30 metres.

Some kilometres before Sainte-Engrâce, the path nose-dived into a steep, narrow gully that was running with water. It was really a stream, and was muddy, stony, and so narrow in places that there wasn't even the width to pause with my feet together. If I stopped I had to adopt an uncomfortable, unbalanced feet-fore-and-aft stance.

The pièce de résistance for many metres was a tall herbaceous border of nettles on each side which overhung this obstacle course. The nettles had perfected a strategy of hooking onto a brandished Leki pole, running down the length of it, delivering their venom, and then retreating back into the horde so that I couldn't determine which one to attack for revenge. I was furious and lashed out with a curse on many occasions. This section needed some serious upkeep and I decided to write a letter of complaint to the French government.

I eventually burst like a maniac onto the D113 from the region of the Gorges de Kakouéta. I was red-faced with an even distribution of white nettle-rash, and ready for a plane home. Not for the last time.

The night's rest was supposed to be a short distance from here, but it turned out to be what seemed like several miles, though in truth it was no more than two or three. I set off up the gradient – an uphill stretch is the last thing you need at the end of the day – with my eyes half shut so that I could conjure up the impression of a large beer just on the edge of my vision to keep me moving. I used many ploys like this.

There now occurred another encounter with a dog, but one with a difference. A short way along the road I was met by a black and white collie (sheepdog or border type) coming towards me. In spite of my bad mood from the beating that I'd taken from the nettles earlier, and, in spite of a worrying twinge from my left knee that had induced an almost imperceptible limp, I made the mistake of greeting the dog with a cheerful bit of English. I suppose I should have addressed him in French.

"Hello boy, where are you off to then?" I said rather foolishly.

I was about to try to stroke the beast, when I remembered that they have rabies over here. The dog, in return, may also have been put off by my red and white-pimpled blotched face which must have looked like a death-cap toadstool, for it circled warily out to the right and seemed for just an instant to limp. It also watched the poles warily, although I hadn't made any threatening gesture.

Now, instead of continuing down the road, it quickly doubled back and maintained pace with me, just in front and out of range of the poles. Smart dog, I thought. I wandered into another reverie as I walked, and I decided that it had come to meet me and that it was leading me to the gîte d'étape.

Pays Basque Est, Pyrénées-Atlantiques

My first regret at ever having seen this dog happened when a group of walkers approached, and the dog, unbelievably beginning to limp in an exaggerated way, went towards them with his head down and with a very tired, sorry look on his face. The walkers were French, and they stopped and patted the dog without hesitation, roughing his ears, and cupping his face in their hands – his eyes were tight shut in ecstasy. I guess they all have rabies shots over here, like we have jabs for measles or whatever in England.

There were several exclamations such as a long drawn out, "*ahhhhhh, le pauvre...,*" (poor little fellow...) from the mother, and a purse-lipped, two-open-hands-to-the-sky, and very Gallic, "*il est trôp fatiguééé...,*" (he's too tired...) from the short, bullet-headed father. I was just considering and elaborating in my mind about how the lady began her statement with a drawn out sigh, and the man finished his statement like that, and whether the stress in the sentences could be reversed, when I was approached and quizzed on what had happened to the poor animal to make him limp like that.

"He should be resting in his condition," or something like it in French was muttered by another onlooker. I thought that these remarks and the sympathy might have been more appropriately addressed to me, but then I was English and the dog was French.

Remembering, and smiling at one of my favourite scenes from an Inspector Clouseau, Pink Panther film, I explained that it was not my dog and that we'd been thrown together by fate. As I spoke I noticed that they were unable to keep eye contact with me. They would look at me, their eyes flickered across my face, and then they had to look away. I searched for the word leprosy in French so I could reassure them I didn't have it; and I searched for the word for nettle-rash so I could assure them that I did; but my vocabulary didn't stretch that far.

From more shrugs and gestures there then developed the clear impression that because we were so obviously walking together, the dog had become my responsibility anyway. I wondered if there were any legal minds present – the French legal system, unlike ours, takes the view that the accused is guilty until proved innocent.

I could tell that I was now labelled not walker, but *traveller*, with all the sometimes prejudiced, though rarely undeserved distaste for the evidence they leave behind. As the French family continued down the hill, glad to be out of the presence of a parasite such as myself, I looked at the dog and wondered if we could make a living begging in the markets. He just stood there looking back at me, and I could tell he was waiting for me to make the first move. I was becoming just a little suspicious of his motives, and it occurred to me that people might pay heavily just to make us go away.

By this time I'd maybe over-imaginatively christened the by no means unimaginative dog.

He was going to be known as *Mister Blair*.

It was unfortunate that the mongrel had waylaid me on the road. If we'd been on a mountain track our brief encounter might have been different – there would have been fewer opportunities for him to act the goat and get me in trouble. I might then have christened him something more respectable, such as Rover, Spot, or even Saint Francis.

Once our bond – my bondage – was complete the creature had increased his lead to about twenty five metres up the road, and was bounding along with no sign of a limp. There were of course no witnesses to his deception.

Along this part of the route a vertical cliff rose directly on the left side of the road and a steepish slope fell away down to a fast-flowing river on the right. I was proceeding well with the image of imminent refreshment in mind when, around a bend ahead, an old Citroen 2Cv appeared. It was noisily chugging along on a badly maintained engine. There are many like that in France, in spite of a generous government scheme to subsidise their replacement with new vehicles and thereby blatantly subsidise the French motor industry – contrary to all EEC rules. Anyway, the soft top on this one was peeled back, and the car was driven by an elderly man with, presumably, his wife in the passenger seat.

As they were almost drawing level with *Mister Blair*, the dog, without any warning signs, ran from our side of the road directly towards the nearest front wheel of the approaching car in an apparent attempt to snatch the tyre from the rim of the wheel. Practising this tricky manoeuvre was undoubtedly how he had obtained the memory of what a limp should look like. I heard a distinct scream from the elderly passenger, and the driver swerved violently towards the cliff wall, just recovering his line in time to avoid disaster. He then veered over onto my side of the road forcing me to dive onto the grass and narrowly avoid tumbling down the bank and into the river. The car regained its side of the road again, and fortunately there was no other traffic at the time.

Now, Citroen 2CVs were designed to be able to cross a ploughed field carrying a box of eggs – without breaking the eggs. That is a fact. One of the results of this design aim was a very soft suspension, and this car must have been one of the early prototypes with a very very soft version, because it continued down the hill still rolling like a ship with no keel in a storm. The look of malevolence that I noticed on the driver's face, well in one eye anyway, as he glanced at me didn't particularly register at the time. I could only see one eye because as a result of the swerving his typically French beret had slipped down over the other. He must have summoned all of his manual dexterity and monocular vision to keep both car and occupants out of the river.

Two more cars suffered the same treatment, and the second driver slowed right down and shouted at me from the open window.

"Idiot!"

I realised that they too had assumed that the clown in front was with me.

I now tried to get past the liability and leave him behind, but every time I got close or drew level he'd look at me, flatten his ears, limp slightly, and then leap ahead with all the agility of a dog half his age. If the joker had been bigger I would have sworn it was someone dressed up, it was so crafty.

I eventually got my chance and seized it.

When another unsuspecting pair of victims stopped to drool and coo over the limping *Mister Blair* that was giving it his best, the opportunity was too good to miss. He'd added whining and grizzling to the show. I'm certain the man was just about to ask me what had caused the limp, and that he was reaching in his pocket for a coin, when, with *Mister Blair* distracted and with his eyes shut as he enjoyed the attention, I scuttled past as fast as my shattered frame would allow and, with a crazy laugh, I shouted out in English.

"He's all yours, watch out for the cars."

I should have kept quiet, because as I legged it up the road, *Mister Blair* realised his mistake and came bounding after me, all disabilities forgotten – again. With the French couple watching agog, I turned at bay, raised the poles in outstretched arms and, whilst attempting to span the entire narrow road, I waved the poles and again shouted out in English as loud as possible.

"You're not coming past, get back you bugger!"

For the next mile or so I had to be on my guard constantly and was obliged to repel several attempts to get past. I even threw a couple of stones down the road to deter the troublemaker. I felt very bad about that, because although I didn't aim at him, he eventually got the message, and each time I threw a stone or shouted at him he flattened his ears and crouched down at the side of the road. I'd been conned by a dog, I told myself, but I still felt guilty about terminating our companionship.

The final release from his persecution was when another long distance walker came in the opposite direction, and went on down the hill. As they disappeared into the distance *Mister Blair* was now in the lead again with another victim – his limp was back and I'm sure I was already forgotten.

As I continued up the hill I noticed my own limp was getting worse, but when I tried flattening my ears I found it was impossible.

I finally got to the gîte d'étape, and knew that there had been no choice about getting rid of the dog; how would I have been received if I'd been accompanied by a schizophrenic dog with Tourette's Syndrome? Two exposures to Tourette's Syndrome within a fortnight surely cannot be co-incidence I thought, and I wondered if it had jumped the species in France and might be on the point of spreading throughout the world.

Talking with Klaus later that evening over a beer, I casually introduced the subject into the conversation.

"You didn't have any odd encounters with dogs today by any chance?" and he told me he had passed a French walker going down the hill who seemed to be unwillingly in the company of a black and white sheepdog with a limp. He thought it wasn't an entirely happy arrangement because the other walker kept lunging wildly at it with a stick, and kept shouting *"Merde!"*

I knew how he felt.

Mister Blair had selected at least three separate victims that day, but Klaus and the dog had apparently ignored one another. It's a complete mystery as to how he selected his victims. I wondered if he had a fetish for self-opinionated rucksacks, or if he disliked Germans.

What an excellent gîte d'étape at Sainte-Engrâce – magnificent garbure in the small restaurant, followed by piperade, chicken, and ice-cream.

The quiet village is surrounded by high horizons of forest, and is blessed with intriguing views up steep-sided rocky gorges – mysteries that curve away into the densely wooded remoteness. There is a fascinating ancient little church with many very old headstones shaped like Celtic crosses. I wondered about the extent of the contacts of the old inhabitants with their immediate neighbours in the Pyrénées, how wide the ancient civilisation spread, and where it came from originally and when; gradual migration over many thousands of years I felt.

Day 13: Sainte-Engrâce to La Pierre Saint-Martin
10:30 – 17:00

Today I would leave the Basque country and enter the region of Béarn, doggy experiences would be fewer and more mature, but I was about to enter what my guide-book calls *really big mountain country*. I didn't like the sound of that. The Basque and Béarn regions are both part of the Pyrénées-Atlantiques, but distinct; and Béarn is more mountainous.

Klaus had departed before me, along with one of the Swiss, but the other two Swiss were late risers that morning. About twenty of us had spent the night in quite a large dormitory. Very comfortable, and I didn't remember any snoring. Perhaps I got the prize last night.

After an initial small descent the ascent away from Sainte-Engrâce was a nightmare again. Up, up through woods, slightly east of southeast. A long climb up a boulder-strewn ravine, and my left knee was giving real trouble. Klaus was somewhere ahead – a couple of miles probably – and the two Swiss would be not far behind.

At 13:30 I arrived at an elaborately painted water trough with a bizarre sculptured face next to it. It was near a line which is quite distinct on all ascents – the point at which the trees were just beginning to thin out. I found a note on the trough from Martin, the first of the Swiss, to his two friends, and I was taking a break when they arrived. They read the note, and we sat and enjoyed the tranquillity together.

Before they were ready to depart I set off up the hill and, not long after this and just after leaving the tree line, I found Martin almost asleep with his boots off. He was reposing under just about the last tree before the long, rocky, bare expanse that led to a distant high ridge. He nodded, yawned, and said something rather indistinct, but which sounded rhetorical and without the need for any particular response.

"What's life for if we can't take a nap in the mountains now and again?"

I smiled and made some sound of agreement and carried on.

Until I'd left the ravine and the trees behind everything had been more than clammy, it had been soaking wet; and then beyond the tree cover the sky became the deepest blue, and the unveiled sun glared down without mercy – and it was hot.

Although all three Swiss were now behind me, though not far, I struck out, determined to get to the next gîte first. There was a series of very wide (more than one hundred metres) zigzags, backwards and forwards up a fairly open rocky hillside, and I kept looking back to see if the pursuit was in sight. I didn't want to give away the direction, since it had taken me one or two traverses to locate the *ballises*, although the general bearing was not in doubt. There was no ill-feeling, but I thought *there're three of them – let them find the way.*

I was only a couple of hundred metres or so below the final ridge in front, when all three Swiss came into view about a mile away and far, far below. They were moving quickly with their fast-pacer Martin leading. I was now the quarry, and they were the hunters. This was a great diversion, and I laughed – *hang on* I thought, *I'm actually enjoying this.*

As I climbed towards the ridge that I knew was going to be the Col de la Pierre Saint-Martin, on the frontier with Spain, I was completely unprepared for the revelation that was about to take place. I hadn't seen much snow up till now; I'd seen some small patches below the tree line in north-facing hollows, but that was all. Since Hendaye the terrain had been steep at times, and wooded, and hot. As I crested the Col I found out why I was here. This point in the book would have been better presented in *Imax* cinema form, or as a multimedia book with an increasingly stereophonic, full orchestral backing.

The view to the east for many miles, from the north to the south, was a series of snow fields stretching out among woods and mountains, and the whole view was dominated by the awesome Pic d'Anie. From this angle the Pic d'Anie had a triangular profile, and it looked just like the dorsal fin of a cosmic shark, passing through mountainous seas from left to right, just over the horizon. See the back cover of this book. I just gaped, then I took off my rucksack so that I could relax and take it all in. I took a photograph, and after some chocolate, an orange (the peel of which I hid under a low bush), and an unknown period of time during which I just looked in a dream to the east, I suddenly became aware of the Swiss approaching. Damn, they'd sneaked up and almost caught me. Unwilling to have to speak or even be in human company in the presence of that view, I grabbed the rucksack, and fled down the D132 that approached the Col from the east. After hesitantly crossing a small snow field, my first, I got into Saint-Martin first. Well, first after Klaus that is. Molly had passed through two days earlier and had left her address with a request for a card from the end of the trail. This seemed to amuse la Patronne hugely. Regrettably, I left next day and forgot to write it down.

Surprisingly, washing clothes here was frowned on, but I managed to get a bowl of hot water, and I was instructed to rinse the items outside under a tap from the spring. This tap gave the tiniest dribble, and after a lot of waiting I'd just finished when the Swiss arrived. They had also stopped to take in the view from the Col de la Pierre Saint-Martin. They were to take a bus out to return home the next day.

The food here was superb, excellent garbure, filet de faux (sirloin, cooked how you liked it) and spaghetti, followed by fromage, and a desert.

Sitting outside afterwards, beneath a still-blue sky, we were over-awed by the snow-capped Pic d'Anie in front to the east, and also by the views between a gap in the mountains on the left down towards the lower northern lands that were totally covered by cloud. At about 1640 metres, we were well above the cloud layer, and with the sun now well below the horizon, for the first time it felt cold. More than just fleetingly so.

Day 14: La Pierre Saint-Martin to Lescun
08:30 – 17:00

This was another eventful day, the sky was clearest blue, and it was baking hot all day – awful. I missed or rather lost the track three or four times as I struggled across the plateau from Saint-Martin. This limestone plateau is known as the Arres de Camlong, and Castle warns that the track can be difficult to follow, and that it can be just downright difficult even when you are following it. He also refers to it as being *dry*. When I was there it was still well-camouflaged with snow as well. The only way across was by compass, a lot of luck, and a lot of shouting and lashing out with the Leki poles.

More than once I found myself clinging to some isolated pine tree on a small hillock, surrounded by snow, and trying to see how I could maintain the compass heading. Most of the *ballises* were covered by snow. I was well off-track and I knew it, but there was no alternative but to cross more depressions and small ravines that cut my line of travel, and to wade through snowfields to get back onto where I expected the track to be.

I sank in snow several times, and I even started a small scree avalanche that knocked me sideways and a few feet down a slope. All the way across the plateau it was so hot, in spite of the snow, that the occasional trees smelled like a sauna – pine resin – and the rocks were almost singing. The reflected heat was terrific and it's only May with snow still around; what's it like in Summer I wondered?

This couldn't continue forever I thought, and I eventually got to the Pas de l'Osque at 1922 metres. The first vertical obstacle of any sort now presented itself, and I had to scale a small and almost vertical rock face about twenty feet. It doesn't sound much, and there were plenty of good foot and hand-holds, but a slip could have caused a rolling / bouncing fall much further with a far from trivial outcome. I'd crossed many snowfields to get this far and there was no going back. I carried on over a ridge, and on to Pas d'Azuns at 1873 metres. From this point there is a hair-raising view of the famous twin-peaked Pic du Midi d'Ossau in the far distance. I found it quite sinister, and all this time the Pic d'Anie is towering over the humble explorer on the right hand side. It was awesome.

Somewhere along the track I stopped and drank untreated snow melt water from a rushing tributary of the Aspe, it was so very cool and refreshing – and I had a great feeling of being close to the mountains, though why this should have only now occurred to me I don't know, since I'd been in the wretched things for some time.

On and on, descending over stony, rocky tracks. At one lower point I was stopped by a group going in the opposite direction who complemented me on my descent. They said they'd spied me on the distant summit and were impressed at how I'd fairly run down the boulder-strewn track. I felt a little foolish, but continued to plummet past some now-empty cabannes at about 1689 metres, and arrived exhausted at the refuge de Labérouat at 1442 metres. It was closed, there was no water there, and no hiding place. I was again totally fed-up at this point – my knee was very bad, and I was limping all the time now. I realised that I'd lost the discipline that is vital to achieve maintainable progress.

As I rounded a sharp bend and came into the line of sight from a lay-by where the road terminated – or from my point of view began – I was whacking the occasional nettle with the pole, and I think I might have shouted at one that got me on the hand.

I'd only gone another couple of paces and I looked up at the characteristic sound of a car's central locking system. I had surprised a lone couple in a car, and in terror they had locked their door. I must have looked worse than I felt, and I wondered if Tourette's Syndrome was contagious, and what the incubation period might be.

There was no gîte d'étape before Lescun and although it was only supposed to be less than an hour, I looked at the map to see if I could find water earlier. Even with a can of coke (a trick learned from Molly) in addition to my normal two and a half litres of water at the start, I'd almost run out, and I thought it best to replenish before it went entirely. So I now began to look out for water in earnest.

There was nothing – Alan Castle was quite right to describe it as *dry*.

I have been known to have one-for-the-road at my local pub before setting off on the quarter mile trek home, and I was uncomfortable at the thought of an unslakable thirst. I hate thirst.

LESCUN – lovely – water troughs / taps everywhere. The sound of running water and the sight of ornamental basins overflowing with clear, cool, turbulent oceans of the precious substance was indescribable. I thought it was a really welcoming place and I couldn't resist the urge to plunge my head into one of the elaborately carved stone basins of cool delight.

Head dripping, cooled and refreshed, I set off to find accommodation but found the gîte d'étape in town closed – it was another Hostellerie de Montagne – like Chalet Pedro – and not open yet. If Klaus had been here we could have set his hat and scarf as bait and we might have caught us a kind and obligated guardienne.

Feeling that I'd at least made an effort to get into a lower cost gîte I now turned to the Hôtel de Pic d'Anie – which I secretly wanted anyway – and hoped that there would be vacancies. Yes, I'm in for two nights relaxation and recovery among the water features. There is also a gîte d'étape attached to the hotel as in Castle, and I think that I'd spotted it before going into the hotel, but sometimes the heart has to rule the head.

As I sat with a beer at a roadside table at the hotel before actually booking in I heard a familiar voice behind me. It was Klaus. There was some badinage, and I considered asking if I could borrow his hat and scarf for a while; but then I thought the memory of Chalet Pedro might still be too painful.

He was also booked in here, so I thought there will be a pleasant few hours over a meal later and asked him what he wanted to drink. The waiter was standing at our side so Klaus pointed across the small street to a table in the shade where two girls were sitting with drinks – I always prefer to bake in the sun a little more at the end of the day – and he enquired of the waiter in French.

"What is that green fish over there, I think I would like one."

The waiter and I both looked at Klaus, then at each other. I looked over at the girls, and my first thought was that neither of the girls looked particularly fishy or green, and secondly I thought that perhaps Klaus should get out of the sun; but the waiter had the answer.

"Pas *poisson*, Monsieur, c'est une *boisson*." Klaus had seen a Diabolo Menthe – lemonade with green mint syrup – and he had used the French word *poisson* – fish, instead of the similar sounding *boisson* – drink. Very childish to laugh at I'm sure, but unfortunately the two girls thought we were laughing at them and referring to them as green fish. They got up and flounced off in a huff. Pity really.

When I got up to go inside and book in, I was more than just a little stiff after the relaxation at the outside table, and I puffed, stretched a bit, and groaned when I took hold of a strap, and picked up the corporate beast of a rucksack that had been lurking in the shadow behind us. Klaus said something when he saw my resentment towards my rucksack.

"You poor old bugger, let me take that," and he reached for it, lifted it, and then put it back down.

"What the hell have you got in this, it's half as heavy again as mine! Here, you take it!"

I think he was surprised by the dead weight and malevolence of it. I tried to explain that the rucksack was beyond my control, and that I thought it was surreptitiously gathering things to itself as I carried the damn lazy thing all the way. It never ever returned the favour by carrying me in return.

He then suggested that perhaps we could shoot it, and I said that was a typical German response, and anyway we didn't have a gun. He did, in fact, very kindly carry it upstairs for me while I checked in.

I'd come closest yet to running out of water today, I actually had about one half litre in reserve. I was very worried about my left knee – it could ruin everything – but I hoped that a day off might fix it. Otherwise I would have carried on the next morning. It was seven days since my last rest day, but apart from the knee, things were not too bad. The elasticated bandage today didn't eliminate the problem, and it had caused bad chaffing behind the knee.

Now, in my mind, the area of the Aspe equates to Bears, they use the Vallée d'Aspe as one of their Pyrénéan crossing routes. I made a mental note to get the chilli and knife sorted out.

Selected Photographs Pay Basque Est

Day 10 – 23 May 15:06
Scattered skeletal remains of the Cromlechs on the Sommet d'Occabé.

Day 11 – 24 May 09:40
Chalet Pedro the morning after the crime. The hat, scarf, and guidebook
belonging to Klaus were mauled on the chairs outside the restaurant.

Day 12 – 25 May 10:01
The Passerelle d'Holzarté Bridge – don't look down.

Day 13 – 26 May 10:22
Ancient headstones at the church at Sainte-Engrâce.

Day 13 – 26 May 11:03
On the way to the Col de la Pierre Saint-Martin.

Day 14 – 27 May 12:58
First sight of the awesome Pic du Midi d'Ossau from the Pas d'Azuns at 1873 metres. The unmistakable cleft peak is in the centre. I shivered.

Day 14 – 27 May 21:45
The moon keeping a respectful distance as the Pic d'Anie peers menacingly over a darkening Lescun.

5   Béarn, Pyrénées-Atlantiques, Hautes-Pyrénées
     Day 15: Rest At Lescun

I had a very quiet rest day at Lescun.

I said goodbye to Klaus and I did not see him again. I'd enjoyed his company immensely and was a little sad to see him go. He was going to pick his car up in Cauterets, and that would be the end of his jaunt this year. He later sent Lesley some photographs he had taken and a very friendly letter referring to our escapade.

I cleaned my boots (yet again) and I waxed them (yet again) – they looked like new. I was later to regret all the cleaning effort – it had been considerable.

The small church in the village was very Catholic and medieval in character, and there was a small horse-drawn hearse in an annex. I wondered how often they needed it. A lot of these delightful Pyrénéan villages are dying, along with their ageing residents, as younger people leave for the cities and never return.

I took a good tour of the village which took about twenty minutes. I bought tuna, bread, some raisins, an apple and orange, and two Mars bars.

I really must get rid of that bag of peanuts that I have portered since Hendaye, I thought. If I can find it that is. It's never in the same place twice. I always put it in with the other food that I'm carrying, but by the end of the day it's somewhere else entirely. And it's not just during the day that it gets about. I even found it in my wash bag on top of my toothbrush one morning. I resolved to set a trap for it that night. If the hauntings hadn't started at home I would have suspected that the peanuts were the cause. They definitely had to go.

I revelled in the very clean, clear water from the many troughs and spring pipes scattered through Lescun. They gave the place an incredibly invigorating and refreshing atmosphere. Outside the church, I met two English walkers with a small dog. Sarah, Jim, and Dougal, a smallish, gentle-looking, pointy-faced black mongrel. (I hope he doesn't mind being called gentle or a mongrel). They were all camping some way lower down the hill from where Lescun is situated and it was quite a climb from the campsite up to Lescun for supplies. They had also walked from Hendaye, and intended going all the way to Banyuls-sur-Mer. While I chatted to Jim and Sarah, Dougal stood very placidly just glancing around at the village – I thought he seemed very relaxed and in tune with it, but I acknowledged that it must have seemed a long way on those little legs.

Day 16: Lescun to Borce
08:00 – 16:00

I managed, with some difficulty to dispose of the peanuts this morning, although they strung the issue out for half an hour or more. The trap that I'd set the night before had been triggered, but it was empty. No surprise there, they were very cunning. The trap was a Leki pole balanced on a waste paper basket. The basket was already in the room, I didn't bring one with me. Silly really to forget such a thing, though I suspected there might be one somewhere in the rucksack by this time – we had seen enough of them on the journey. (By we, I mean the Rucksack and I). There might even be a selection in there; I imagined them as a nest, like Russian Dolls, only very plain-looking – some would be slightly frayed baskets, but there would also be one or two battered and dented grey steel ones like they have in offices.

So, with some confidence, I placed the trap at the entrance to the bathroom. I knew that they were not already in the bathroom when I went to bed because I searched it thoroughly. My intention was to lure them where it suited me, by arranging the wash bag with the toothbrush just cheekily peeping out of the top. I'd placed this alluring sight so that it was just visible from the other side of the room where I'd gathered absolutely everything else, like I always do, ready for packing the next morning. This had the bonus that it ensured that all potential hiding places were separated by a clear area of floor – a killing ground I thought – though if everything went according to plan, I didn't expect to need it. The plan was that the Leki pole would be triggered like a spike by anything trying to enter the bathroom during the night. There were then three possible results, the intruder might be harpooned by the pole, it might be trapped in the waste paper basket, or, it might get into the bathroom, where, if I was quick enough, I could contain it. The noise should wake me. I'd already made sure that the bathroom window was locked so it could not easily or quickly get out that way.

Thoughts of escaping from a window then made me wonder if the current quarry could have been responsible for arranging my Pyrénéan guide book in such a scary fashion in the hotel at Hendaye, but I realised that the peanuts had a pretty good alibi – they were still in the shop at that time. I thought when I bought them that the shopkeeper seemed glad to get rid of them to me, I think they had probably been giving him trouble for some time. Perhaps if I caught them intact I could post them back to him from Lescun. That would be quite a shock, and I'd like to see his face as he unwrapped the parcel and understood the cruel twist of fate. On second thoughts I don't ever want to see his face again, it was like a smoked kipper with a hat on – sort of flat and yellowish, with the eyes almost on the side of his head where his ears should be.

Anyway, I'm digressing. When I awoke and saw the sprung trap, I expected to find the peanuts in the bathroom, so I ran in and shut the door behind me. I almost tripped over the Leki pole on the way, and noticed that the basket had taken on a hideous shape, and that it looked as though someone or something, possibly about the size of a rucksack, had sat on it. There must have been quite a struggle during the night I thought, it's odd that I was not woken by it. The rucksack appeared to be asleep, in more or less the same place that I'd left it the previous night, but then I was always the first to go to bed, and it was *always* in more or less the same place – too predictable I thought.

I was expecting to have no difficulty apprehending the nuts, and thought that if I could knock them into the bath I might be able to drown them. The bathroom of course was empty, although the toothbrush looked as though it had been briefly interfered with, and I got the impression that the attacker had been disturbed.

After a lot of searching, during which there were rustlings and scrapings, and during which I thought it was hiding in places I'd already searched, so that I frequently had to go back and do a re-search, I finally found it, looking a lot smaller than when I'd bought it. It was in the container that I use for the maps of ground that I've already covered, and that I do not need any more. Now I know that I did not put them there, but at least I now had them. I managed to substitute the horribly flattened basket with the closest match from the now expansive stock in the rucksack, and placed the bag of nuts in the bottom, with the remnants of the original basket on top.

Leaving Lescun I reset my pedometer as I'd done every day so far, so that at the end of the day I would have all sorts of statistics on the day's horrors. I limped off, my right leg was sore as well now; it was as if something had stabbed it during the night. Shortly down the trail, I took a look at the pedometer and found that it was not working reliably. All my records to this point were therefore unreliable and so I stopped using it. This was very disappointing since I had carefully calibrated my length of step before I left home, had given some thought as to how it would be affected by other than level walking, and the data I had collected *every* day up to now was as follows:

1. Distance covered
2. Time spent in motion
3. Average speed
4. Number of steps
5. KCals burned

Of course it's really all based on just the mechanical joggling that it gets, and elapsed time. The rest depends on body weight and length of stride. Some would say, and some walkers did say, what a strange thing to want to do. Well, I thought, it is no stranger than wanting to punish oneself by walking in mountains. I recorded the information because it interested me and I was very sorry that such a souvenir of the adventure was now denied me.

Ascents today were not too bad and water was freely available on the route. As I was walking across the plateau known as Lhers, where there was plenty of tree cover, and scattered farms, without dogs, I stopped to rest, and looking down I found that the sole of my left boot was literally coming off. This was very worrying and depressing, especially considering the terrain of the next two to three days. I'd not noticed it when I cleaned the boots only yesterday.

I finally got to Borce after falling headlong down a path after turning to read a sign without stopping. I seriously wondered if the loose boot sole might have contributed. This fall had been stupid; in uneven terrain the eyes have to be constantly scanning the underfoot surface, that is one unfortunate fact about walking in the mountains, it is often impractical to try and take in the beauty of the surroundings. When forging ahead, the day's memories are of an undulating, textured, grey and brown ribbon. It's only by taking lots of time that the views can be appreciated. That's one of the reasons why I move so slowly, I flattered myself.

Anyway, when I hit the ground, hard I might add, something in the rucksack also hit me from behind. My first thought was that the peanuts had either managed to stow-away in spite of my vigilance, or that they'd stalked me and pounced on me from behind. I was so incensed, that I lay on the ground for some time beating it with a Leki pole and screaming blue murder at it – the ground that is. When I suddenly realised there might be others about, watching this demented assault on planet Earth, I feigned death for a while, squinting from one eye to see if anyone was there. I ended up in a fit of hysterics over how ludicrous the whole damn thing was becoming.

The shop attached to the gîte at Borce opened specially for three of us – the guardienne thought that she had some *Col* – glue – that might fix my boot, but I was very disappointed when she found that she had sold out. There was again plenty of water in local water troughs, and dozens of bees servicing the thriving local honey industry.

Over my meal of soup, sardines, bread and apple I chatted with the other two residents at the gîte, which I remember as being spotlessly clean. They were pèlerins – pilgrims, and on a pilgrimage to Spain. I shared some wine with them, and we toasted everyone's pèlerinage – whatever their motivation. The telephones in the village were said to be cut off, but I managed with difficulty to get a line home, and to start the boot replacement saga running.

It had been a roasting hot day, all sun, and very bad walking apart from the shade through the plateau de Lhers.

Day 17: Borce to Refuge D'Ayous
08:00 – 17:00

I started the day very depressed at the prospect of a possibly very hard and long stage. Will the boot last? What am I going to do if the sole comes off completely miles from anywhere? What is the Chemin de la Mature going to be like? and what about my left knee and right ankle which really were both giving me trouble? My back was still not right either, though I suspected that maybe for the first time in years it was actually feeling stronger. I tied some paracord round the flapping sole and, feeling more like a gentleman of the road – an English tramp – than ever, I set off.

Down into the Valle d'Aspe – no bears about thank goodness – and through Etsaut. I saw the pèlerins waiting for a bus here, cheats, and off due south, parallel with the main N134 road which climbs eventually to the Col du Somport, and then goes over the border into Spain.

Just outside Etsaut I saw some faded graffiti in large letters on a cliff-face, it read *Non a l'Ours* – No Bears! I definitely go along with that, I just hope that they can read. This was actually a reference to moves that the French government has made during the last decade or so to try and reverse the shameful persecution and decline in numbers of brown bears over the last century. They have attacked the problem by importing Czech brown bears. Farmers, in spite of generous compensation schemes for lost livestock, are very much against the scheme. Although the graffiti was faded, it is very much a live issue as I found out later.

At the start of the Chemin de la Mature I paused to look down at the Fort du Portalet where the road went through a very narrow tree-lined cutting as it climbed on its way south. From much further below in the distance I could clearly hear heavy lorries changing down through gears to assault the slopes.

The Fort was an interesting relic, and I thought I recognised it from a couple of paintings by Turner that I'd seen at an exhibition in London not long before. One of the paintings showed it (or a very similar one) strewn with military casualties, it would have been a nightmare fighting there. It's a nightmare just standing here looking at it. It doesn't appear to be a tourist target and I wondered if it was now in private hands.

The Chemin de la Mature is an impressive notch cut into the side of a virtually sheer mountainside. As you walk up from Borce it is overhung by the mountain from above on the left (north-ish) side. Below the Chemin the mountain falls very steeply, sheer in places, on the right (south-ish, towards Spain). Although it is generally wide enough to pass other walkers, and there is enough headroom to walk upright, it is a memorable experience. It is quite steep in places, and care is required. The fact that it was once used to transport timber from forestry activity higher up I found hard to believe.

After a short distance it curved more directly to the east and became very hot with the sun shining directly down the cutting. Leaving the Chemin de la Mature, and now fully open to the roasting sun, there was a lengthy trek of some hours to eventually arrive at the Col de la Hourquette de Larry at 2055 metres.

On the way there was occasional shade in woodland, and in one of these I was trying to cross a swollen river when I went in up to the knees and I could not get out until my feet were totally soaked. Thankfully, drinking water was also freely available throughout. It was an awful, awful drag to the Col de la Hourquette de Larry – the last stage being a very steep approach across slippery grass because the path was blocked by snow. It was on this final approach to the Col that I first encountered the Davy Crockett hats that seemed to be everywhere, squeaking and running in all directions. They turned out to be marmots.

Just when the ordeal seemed to be over, I realised that there was still the next Col before the descent to the refuge for the night. A typical scenario.

It was 16:00 and I was just approaching the Col d'Ayous – 2200 metres – and wondering *what if the other side is snow-blocked. Although it's south-facing, it's still very early in the year?*

I reached the Col, looked over and – what a nightmare – it was.

Hundreds of metres of snowfields with no way around them; a vertical descent through them seems to be the only way. Just as I was considering this literal *impasse*, a French guy in shorts suddenly came into sight from higher up to the left. Unbelievably, he was jogging along the peaks. He told me that he was just trotting round the harder rocky ground for a couple of hours and he was surprised that I'd come such a distance from Borce alone. He assured me that the descent should be OK, and so, after a Mars bar, off I went across an untrodden region high in a relatively deserted area – sliding and slipping – and occasionally losing a leg through the snow into a rushing river beneath.

These concealed torrents were a danger of which I'd absolutely no knowledge – I couldn't see them on any map – I'd no idea where they were going, and I wondered whether I was going to go even deeper next time. It was all fairly normal stuff if you're used to this sort of thing. I was not, and probably most people aren't either if the trek is done a little later in the year when the snows have cleared. This was early in the season and it was quite simply treacherous on several sections.

Fortunately, after one of the longest hours in my life (day 17 hadn't yet arrived), the Refuge d'Ayous came into sight below, and I abandoned the idea of getting to lac de Bious-Artigues today.

Getting to the refuge without much more trauma I looked inside. It was low-ceilinged and very dark. There were no lights or electricity, and there was a pervasive smell of old socks and decay; and sleeping happened, if you were blessed, on wooden platforms with foam mattresses. This was not for the faint-hearted. I used one of the foam mattresses. Blankets were also available, but although I made an attempt to catch one, they were too quick.

It was during one of these attempts to snare a blanket that I noticed the figure wrapped up in the corner. It was only 17:00, and this guy was either fast asleep – or worse! I have no idea how long he had been there, and I wondered how often the refuges were inspected. In the cold weather he might have been there months. I was greatly relieved to hear a grunt and a snore, and then regretted it. He'd got the prize that night and it wasn't even dark yet. I blame him for what happened next. In the gloom I spotted what looked like a tired old blanket that appeared to have lost concentration for a moment, (they were all tired and old really). I dived at it, banged my head really hard on a low beam, and sank to the floor – right in a puddle of melted snow just inside the door. With stars literally before my eyes, and a wet bum to go with my wet feet, I shouted, the figure in the corner shot upright – the fool – hit his head on a beam above his bunk and sank back without a sound. That's one way of getting the prize back, I thought, and I kept as still as possible in the dark so that if he came round in the next few seconds he wouldn't know who had shouted.

When I took my boots off to dry them I found my feet were all white and wrinkled from their soaking earlier, so I put my rugged walking sandals on to allow my feet to dry as well. The blankets seemed to have disappeared with the agility of cockroaches – I still remembered the one from Sare and how quickly it could move.

So, back outside I looked around and found eau potable gushing from a plastic pipe sticking up in the air. Tea-time.

I chatted with some Spanish walkers who were doing the circuit of the Pic du Midi d'Ossau, and they told me they had stayed at a refuge at the Lac de Pombie and recommended it. There were also French walkers, and a fine stout-hearted and bearded lone English walker.

Thon à la Catalane (Tuna), cheese, shallots, bread – a stale stretchy baguette of course – raisins, dates, apple and a double-strength cold teabag brew.

Following this small and unrehearsed out-of-the-sack feast, I sat and took in the breathtaking scene of the Pic du Midi d'Ossau reflected in the Lac Gentau which was the first of the series of the Lacs d'Ayous.

Lac Gentau was just below me at 1947 metres, and all of the guide books say this is not to be missed – I most certainly second that.

For no obvious reason at all I thought to myself *It's good to go without food for a while*, and then immediately realised I must have flipped.

Day 18: Refuge d'Ayous to Gabas
07:30 – 11:00

Surprisingly, I slept very well in spite of the bang on the head, or perhaps because of it, and I got up with the dawn at about 06:30. My boots were still not properly dry, but it was just a bit too rough underfoot for the sandals. I had a Mars for breakfast, and then naively took my wash kit to find the loo and a basin which was said to be outside somewhere. I'd just made do with sticking my head under the spring outside the hut the night before.

All the steel doors around the outside of the building were locked, and I was just wondering if there actually was any sort of loo, or if people just went off among the rocks, when, looking around on the ground, I perceived that I was standing in the middle of it. Just behind the refuge – small heaps of human droppings and paper – everywhere – disgraceful, disgusting, and totally unnecessary. It was as though many walkers had contrived their own individual mock-cairns. I could only surmise that it was the result of people visiting while the ground was still covered with thicker snow and that what I was seeing had once been invisible beneath a blissfully sanitising layer of snow. With great care I picked my way out of the human minefield and discovered that miraculously I was uncontaminated.

I got an excellent photograph of the sun just rising, and the early morning reflection of the Pic du Midi d'Ossau in the Lac Gentau, last night's photograph did not have the same colour. The Lac noticeably rose in level from the melting snows, even during the relatively short time overnight, and I made a mental note of that – it would prove useful sooner than I thought.

In spite of the beauty, it was a depressing start again with wet feet. At first, the path wound slightly down, sometimes bare, and sometimes snow-covered. Every so often the track was cut by a shallow, slushy stream from snowfields higher up on my left (North).

Beyond Lac Gentau the track dropped more steeply down – into and through the clouds – and then after a while, once below them, it quickly became unexpectedly much cooler – probably because it was damper.

There was another short drop down to Gabas at 1090 metres, and I decided to stay there, clean up, and start really early the next day for the Hourquette d'Arre. That would likely turn out to be a horror story again I thought, and as shown on the map there would be no refuge or shelter of any kind within hours of the remote Hourquette. Many years later my hair still rises at the sound of that name – the Hourquette d'Arre.

Hôtel Le Biscaü – cheese makers as well, and a hotel dog for company while I had a Ricard, a couple of coffees and a beer – I needed it.

I started to plan the next day's adventure – I had a suspicion that really careful planning would be a good idea for the forthcoming section and, as evident from my log at the time, I had a feeling that it was going to be *eventful*.

A small verbatim extract from the log, written in Gabas reads:

> *...Gourette should be some form of breakpoint – will then be in the Haute Pyrénées, and for a while should have more options for breaking the journey. Tomorrow will be a major challenge! Boot deterioration seems to have stabilised – may be chance of repair at Gourette – if snowfields permit.....*
> *Banged head very badly in refuge d'Ayous – jarred neck – almost senseless – neck still stiff today. Left knee still bad, and right ankle feels weak – think I need a holiday.*

So I sat down, and started planning for the next day. I decided that I might well bivvy at about 1643 metres just past the gouffres that were marked on my map, or further on at about 1750 metres where there might be water. The word gouffre translates as gulf, pit or abyss. I didn't like the sound of that. Castle says it is a bad section with poor water supply. I tried to find the mountain guides to determine the conditions on the Hourquette d'Arre but the office was closed.

Had they been open, and had I received the synopsis that I later learned was issued that awful day, I have no idea what I would have done.

At the Refuge d'Ayous, a French chap had told me that the hot weather was totally unusual, and I was now hoping that it might therefore help to reduce the snowfields. I also remembered with some concern, a tale told me by a lady in a walker's shop in our nearby home town of Sherborne. She had recounted how a party of their friends had attempted the GR10, and had been forced to abandon the attempt because of blocked passes in this very region. That had been even later in the year – three or four weeks later.

Meanwhile, in not quite blissful ignorance, mealtime at the Hôtel Le Biscaü was *interesting*. Soup, consisting of what they euphemistically called Japanese pearls in stock, turned out to be savoury sago. Try as I did I could not manage to get the stock without the sago. Every time I had just got a spoonful of liquid alone, a gang of little sago balls would slither, in a rush, into the spoon, and displace half the stock. I wanted to smack the spoon down hard on them but I sensibly refrained. I like sago, but as a pudding, not in the soup. Mixed salad was next – tinned! – it turned out to be what my grandfather used to call *cat spew*. It certainly looked like it. This was followed by couscous, two chorizo slices, plus a quadrant of terrine.

There had been no warning about the soup – it had just arrived. I had thought that there might have been a choice of something light from the carte, but it wasn't to be.

Another couple of large guests who were also imprisoned with me just looked at the soup as if it might suddenly rear up out of the bowl and drench them. They obviously didn't get fat on sago. Something polite was said when the bowl was taken away untouched and spared them the ordeal. I couldn't tell exactly what they said, I think they apologised for leaving it. Maybe they were English.

I finished most of mine, and was rewarded with a beam from the colossal waitress who looked as though she loved sago. I could hear something frying in the kitchen nearby and wondered if they were frying more sago. No, here it comes, it's a rare-fried piece of pork with what looks like crème anglaise – custard. Well, if they put sago in the soup, why not custard on the meat. It was actually very, very runny mashed potato. This was only obvious to the palate when it was spooned directly to the mouth in large quantities using the serving spoon. In small quantities it was quite tasteless, a sort of culinary vacuum or black hole, and it defied all attempts to harvest it with a fork. I surprised the waitress by cleaning all plates and cutlery with bread. They were so clean that she was puzzled and wondered if I'd been served yet. I said that I always ate like that. If the food had been better I could have got away with it and had another lot for free.

Although I was going to have it anyway, I was surprised when the fromage arrived and was banged down without question. Will there now be sago pudding I wondered? – No, the next thing to arrive was just my petit déjeuner on a tray so I can have it in my room and leave early. They did do my washing that consisted of trousers, shirt, all socks, and underwear for next to nothing – three Francs I think.

After the meal I called the waitress over and asked if I could buy some chocolate and an orange to help me get through my journey to Gourette. She said no, and after a pause, during which she gave me a level stare, she added that it would not be a problem since they'd have plenty *in* Gourette. She punctuated the *in* with a sausage-like finger. Now I thought it was pretty clear that I meant I wanted them to eat on the journey – rations for survival. I actually had the survival food already, but I find an orange and chocolate more of a comfort. We both looked a bit blank at her reply, and I swear she was staring me out, daring me to try asking for something else. I held her gaze as long as I could; I'd eaten all the sago, and I had thought that I'd made an ally. At last, as she seemed to grow larger, while the room became smaller and more menacing, and the shadows advanced like a tide towards me, I looked away first. From some remote part of the room, as if by antipodal ventriloquism, there was the smallest evidence of flatulence, and with a smile, she went triumphantly back to the scullery – where she belonged I thought.

Day 19: Gabas to Lac d'Anglas
07:00 – 18:00

The log of this section was written a day late in Gourette on day 20 – for reasons that will become apparent.

Knowing that the day would be severe I started early and walked North up the road, past the still-closed mountain advice centre, and past some holiday accommodation where many wholesome cars were parked. The road climbed slightly, bending more to the east, and the GR10 eventually left it towards the northwest for a while before heading north. So, it was into the wilderness again.

I passed through dripping deserted woods for an hour or more on the way to the Corniche des Alhas. There were black and yellow salamanders galore, and every step brought a spider's web in my face and showers from the sodden trees. This was true virgin rain forest and everything was dark, dank, and thoroughly mysterious as I pushed like a pioneer through the undisturbed undergrowth. It was very misty, cool, and good for walking. After a mile or so it became apparent that the forest had in fact been ravaged. The tracks through the woods became very badly disturbed by logging activities, and *ballises* were suddenly non-existent over long sections. Most careful compass work and luck got me over the first one or two miles or so through the densely wooded hillsides. There were few obviously correct tracks, and absolutely no *ballises*. I stopped many times to take in the still, heavily oppressive, dank atmosphere, and I saw nobody throughout the entire, memorable day. This was why I was here.

The Corniche des Alhas is a track cut into the mountainside, something like the Chemin de la Mature, except that the drop to one side is more often sheer, and it is even narrower, more winding and more tortuous, and simply more – exciting. There is a warning beforehand that it is *Vertigineux* (vertiginous or precipitous) – repeated in Castle. Thankfully there was a chain rail along its outer edge, and so the recurrent tendency to be propelled towards, and bounced over the precipice by the rucksack banging on the overhanging cliff wasn't too bad. It was too misty to see the sheer drop, which may have been a good thing, but regrettably, the reputedly fine views were also blanketed out; and anyway, with hindsight I'd rather have had the opportunity to be awestruck. I was genuinely disappointed at the poor visibility – I might, after all, never pass this way again I thought.

Higher up much of the track had been eroded by snow slides and avalanches, and because it was early in the season it had not yet been repaired. Such sections were truly awful to cross. There would often be a forty five degree plane, or steeper – no level path at all – and the surface was frequently dry, fine and dusty. Below this chute, the stony slope went sometimes even more steeply down, about fifty metres and more at times, into the fast-flowing swollen river. This was insane I thought.

Above the angled chute there was sometimes a mass of scree or loose boulders, or snow – the whole lot looking as though it was just waiting for me.

Later, as a variation, I crossed two rivers that were really too wide to sensibly attempt, but I was damned if I was going back. Run, jump, hit the opposite bank, slide back into the water, drag out. Maniacal laughter and shrieks at times.

Much later (about nine miles?) and higher, after the Chemin Horizontal which is a long and gradually ascending stretch of frequently worn away sections – and not *horizontal* at all – when I was totally exhausted, I was faced with more snowfields and scree slopes leading up to the Hourquette d'Arre.

My real worry at this point was that I could see two possible routes and no *ballises*. I knew that if I went over the wrong ridge and then down what would inevitably be a steep, one-way slide, then I could get both lost and stuck. It could be weeks before this section was sensibly and safely passable. However did I come to be in such a forsaken place.

Standing and waiting for some sort of inspiration, I noticed away on the left slope, some large openings, and after initially thinking I might sleep there, I realised they were probably the ancient mines marked on my map, and that I'd got the correct approach. Taking a couple of compass bearings, and checking the altitude on the wrist-beast, it seemed a reasonable bet that the Hourquette d'Arre was the imposing knife edge straight ahead.

Some parts were north-facing, and there was more snow and ice than I'd yet seen – anywhere, ever. To return would be a nightmare, to go on would be a nightmare. Castle advises avoiding a snow field on the west side of the final approach to the Hourquette, in favour of the scree slope on the east side. When I arrived there both sides were mostly snow-covered, but there was some small evidence of one or two patches of scree amidst the snow on the east slope. I went for the east slope for no reason other than that it looked less steep.

Entering this fairyland, I went diagonally upwards, from sloping snowfield with avalanche evidence and more overhanging snow above, to small inhospitable scree islands, and I repeated this several times. Scree fell away, snow fell away – cascading down in a growing slurry into a bowl of deep loose snow and stones that would have been the end of me if I'd gone with it.

I have since come to the belief that I was traversing the slope lower than the hidden trail. The trail is usually a level track, cut into such a slope. I now believe I was crossing loose scree that was partly bound by a covering of snow, and that I was lucky to get away with it.

Strangely, I wasn't exactly terrified at this time, but all thoughts of humour and taking photographs (regrettably) went out of my mind. It was a case of slow steps, making footholds in the sloping face, and using the trusty poles for support. On more than one occasion, when the slope seemed to tremble, I had to twist round and use both hands and feet to dig into the slope to keep to my position. This was where I needed the crampons and ice-pick that were reposing at home. I knew there was no-one within several miles, no phone signal, and that this really was a time for keeping calm. I think I spoke aloud just once.

"Oh ****, you've really done it now."

It was nearing 17:00 when I realised that although I'd cleared the tricky bit, the swirling mists that had appeared about an hour earlier were getting worse. There would be a brief clear patch, then mist and cloud would literally flow or pour over one of the ridges to the east, rolling down the slope like lava and obscuring everything and making it very cold. This flow of mist was quite awe-inspiring and I recall thinking that it was like a saucepan of milk coming to the boil, when the thick creamy froth rises slowly and overflows the rim. A cup of hot milk would have gone down very nicely.

It was in these circumstances that I found myself straddling the Hourquette d'Arre at 2465 metres and at about 17:30. The sharp edge of an Hourquette is exactly that – a narrow ridge of rock, almost like climbing over a wall, and quite different to a smooth extended, drawn-out grassy Col. I tore the seat of my trousers trying to perch on the ridge. The mist at this time was total. There was a few feet of visibility and that was it. I looked around in this shrunken world and tried to find a place to lie down out of the wind in my bivvy gear. There was barely a safe ledge anywhere, just snow and uneven rock, and I could not safely go back to the area near the caves because it would have meant re-crossing the perilous snow and scree slopes. If necessary, I would have to wrap around one of the rocks and see the night through like that.

Again unsure of the best thing to do, I was helped by a sudden lightening, and brief clearing of the mist. I managed during that one or two minutes to get a compass bearing on what looked like a distant ridge to the northeast, and checked that it was about right on the map. That was enough, sack on and over the Hourquette into the north-facing, gradually sloping but mostly level snow fields. I was very nervous about what I was crossing – mines were marked on the map – and I had no idea what was under the snow. Shafts were a possibility, and since the track way-marks were some feet below the snow, and I was going by compass, I was obviously cutting bends and straying from the invisible track. I thought of the yawning gouffres – bottomless abysses – and my toes literally curled in my sole-flapping boot.

After the longest mile in my life, with thick mist back, and as the light was fading, I stood at the top of a long steep snow field that disappeared down through the mist. I believed that the lac d'Anglas was at the bottom about 1,000 feet below, but I couldn't see it.

At this point I was committed.

I went over the edge and tried to make my way down very, very slowly – I'd no visual confirmation that my map work was correct – there might have been a sheer drop just beyond my vision. I could see nothing but mist below. Early on I rolled down a short distance after losing a pole, and managed to stop the slide by clawing at the snow with my hands, and then had to climb back up to retrieve it. It was difficult to control the descent, and there was a great deal of shouting and cursing. With about 400 feet still to go, I suddenly lost my footing, and with gathering momentum and more cursing I fell another couple of hundred feet towards I knew not what. When I managed to stop I found that I was below the mist, and that a few hundred feet away and below me was a frozen lake. It made me think of one of Gustave Doré's illustrations from Dante's Inferno, although I couldn't quite make out any frozen heads sticking up through the ice.

Standing by the lake however, were two or three people, and they were looking up to where I sat thrashing the snow with the baton Anglais. The relief at this point was overwhelming, and I almost wept. The final slither to the lake was a relative pleasure with no more cursing.

Reaching the bottom I straightened my clothing, beat the snow from my hat, and walked across to what turned out to be a group of fishermen. They'd hiked up the short distance, a mile or so, from the town of Gourette and they were fishing through holes in the ice. They must have stopped to gawp at the apparition which had descended from above the clouds.

"Bonjour Messieurs," I said smiling and, feeling like something of a celebrity, I looked at each in turn and enquired about the name of the lake.

"Quelle est le nom de cet lac?"

They seemed a little awkward at first, and I later realised that they must have heard me cursing high up in the mist before I came into view; and that the appearance of some idiot waving poles, rolling out of the mist, and shouting obscenities in English, was probably the last thing they expected to see at that time of the evening. One of them replied.

"Lac d'Anglas Monsieur."

Now this was really a surprise, because I was ready for a disappointment, but I couldn't show my elation so I just replied in a matter of fact way.

"*Aaah*, bon, comme je croyais," (just as I thought) and I walked off to find a reasonably raised patch of ground on which to sleep. The area was a mass of large puddles and mini lakes.

Dinner consisted of a Mars bar and a handful of raisins. Bed was a relatively complex affair, and that night I slept badly in a double layer of everything, gloves, hat, Gore-Tex jacket, double trousers, double socks, all stuffed into my sleeping bag and bivvy bag. My nose had been badly burned during the day, and the sleeping bag and bivvy bag rubbed and polished it to a fine shade of red / purple during the night. It was a bit nippy but at least I did get some sleep.

When I crawled out of the cocoon the next morning I found that during the night the water around my little island had frozen, and that overall the water levels had risen. My selection of a raised section of ground after seeing the same thing happen at Lac Gentau had paid off.

Day 20: Lac d'Anglas to Gourette
08:30 – 10:35

The pleasure of wet boots to start the day. It was generally overcast – I could have done with some cheery sun. Up and off, and the first hazard was a sloping ice field alongside the lac. I had no crampons or ice-pick and this was a big worry – the slope down into the thawed margin of the frozen lac was smooth hard ice after the night's freeze. I had to rely on the now worn and slippery indentations in the ice that were made by the fishermen the previous day when it was soft, yielding snow. A slip would have taken me through the lightly frozen margin into the freezing water.

The drop down to Gourette after this was uneventful. I passed a young family who were walking up to the Lac d'Anglas and thought how unlikely it would be to see such young children walking in those conditions back home. Gourette was deserted and mostly closed when I got there mid-morning. It was a concrete jungle of out-of-season shops.

I found that my watch was full of condensation, and I had to operate on it at the first bar that I came to in Gourette. I prised off the watch glass with my trusty French Laguiole couteau (pocket knife) – a present from my good friend Jean-Marie – and let the pieces dry out on the table. There was yet another friendly dog here – and this bar seemed like the only one open. Cognac, coffee, water, poulet basquaise (Basque chicken) and chips at 11:30 seemed like a good idea, and I took a tally of the damages so far: broken toothbrush, soles coming off both boots, shoulder strap on rucksack disconnected, trouser seat torn, pedometer unserviceable, watch flooded.

Not unmanageable.

After the dangers of yesterday the rucksack seemed very subdued, and I repaired it as best as I could with a cable tie and some stitching for extra strength. I was not too confident that another part of the strap would last – the strap should really be attached at two points not one like it now is – I must try and relieve it, or get it properly repaired. Cauterets maybe.

I checked in at the Hôtel Glacier, took a really long hot bath, and went back to the bar to see the dog and to take jus d'orange and lemonade. The rucksack stayed in the hotel room.

At 16:40 I checked by phone with Arrens Rando' Plume (the information bureau for the condition of mountain trails), about the route from Arrens to Cauterets. They said OK – *Practicable*. Perhaps I should see what they say about the Hourquette d'Arre. I later did find out from a future walking companion, Jean-Pierre.

Without much else to do, I managed to apply some more strapping to the rucksack to help the weak bit, and it was then completely serviceable, although it was not a very pretty sight.

Still, a blind man would have been glad to see it as they say.

At this time I was actually gaining confidence physically, and I was pleased to think that my back and knee problems seemed to have gone past their worst, and were controllable. I went to sleep that night in what I can only describe as a state of delayed euphoric shock. I was both surprised and glad to be alive.

Day 21: Gourette to Arrens
09:05 – 16:00

Breakfast was the only redeeming feature of the place. I wandered around a totally shut Euro village looking for the GR10 exit to the east and couldn't find it. Eventually I gave up on the map and guide book and followed my instinct back to yesterday's entry point; and of course, there was the exit, ricocheting off the nasty place. The GR10 refused to enter Gourette.

I still find the initial ascent of the day terrible. It's cloudy, misty, a bit cold – good – and after a couple of hours I was looking down to where I would soon join the D918 road for a while – said to be one of the most spectacular roads in France.

I officially crossed the line between the Pyrénées-Atlantiques and the Hautes-Pyrénées at 12:40, and I set the camera to record the auspicious event. My left knee gave way several times on descents although luckily I didn't fall. It's painful now on ascents as well, and I'm very worried that it is the real Achilles heel in the whole business. So much for yesterday's confidence.

14:30 Stopped for lunch – not something I do very often – and had sardines with chilli, bread, and chorizo. After that I felt great again, and made good progress to the outskirts of the destination, where, in the heat and pleasure of the end of the day's ordeal, I had the wonderful treat of a Mars and a Coke from a cosy little shop as I entered Arrens. It seemed a pleasant place, apart from lots of flies, and the gîte d'étape, *Camelat*, looked very good – as did the evening's potential repas. I tried to pick up any voicemail, but the number I'd used many times before was not now recognised, there was no-one at home, and Lesley's mobile was not on – as usual. It later turned out that it was on, but the battery was flat! A classic example of female logic.

In the gîte I spoke with several French people who had been on the route today. It's very pleasant talking about the discomfort after the event. Cyril, a French mountain-biker had passed me earlier, and we chatted in the dortoir (dormitory) and later over a beer about routes and the GR10 in general.

18:00 waiting for the repas that commences at 19:30. There was a group of us huddled in a draughty veranda affair at the back of the gîte. I was making an exhibition of myself swatting flies to keep warm, and I was trying not to drink more beer. The weather was by now decidedly chilly, and I thought that I really needed a pullover or fleece. One of the items I'd posted home would have been very welcome.

18:45 checked with Rando' Plume at Cauterets again. *...little bit of snow but should be no problem – even without crampons.*

If I was going to get into trouble again, I thought, I'd at least go in with my eyes open.

What a phenomenal mealtime. It seems as though half the village has come to eat here – there are three or four tables full – and they certainly are not all staying the night here. There must be thirty people, and everyone is talking at once. There was a big bowl of salad consisting of walnuts, ham, egg, cheese, tomatoes, lettuce... followed by a big bowl of porc – huge chunks plus a great stack of vegetables. This was followed by fromage, and it was all finished off with cassis or myrtille fromage blanc like a knickerbocker glory, oh, and finally fruit. And gallons of red wine of course. I remember nothing after the meal, but I'm sure I slept like a very old, tired oak log.

Breakfast: cereal, yoghurt, orange juice, followed by the usual petit déjeuner – as much as you can eat. Total bill, all-in, including accommodation FFr201 That included beer, and I was given an orange and an apple to take away for the day. I said that I would be back with accomplices. Very pleasant folks, every time a request was made for something, it was met with a smile, and a genuinely friendly response. That's not to say that they ran round like skivvies; everyone was expected to fetch and carry to and from the table, but having good-natured wardens made everything so much more enjoyable.

I didn't realise it at the time, but Lesley and myself had camped at Arrens with our old VW camper van about twenty-five years earlier, with two of our children. She reminded me of this when we returned by car a few weeks after this adventure had finished. Once reminded of the occasion, I clearly remembered standing on the campsite all those years previously, looking at a white cross among the trees on the steep mountainside, and thinking that it would be crazy to invite disaster by maybe getting lost up there. I must have passed within a few hundred feet of that cross without knowing it when I left Arrens the next day.

Béarn, Pyrénées-Atlantiques, Hautes-Pyrénées

Day 22: Arrens to Lac d'Estaing

09:05 – 13:00

This was just a short walk.

Hot, hot, hot under clear skies. There was a thin haze over the sun at the lac – probably just as well. For some while I'd wanted to know why my nose had been getting so badly burned in spite of cream and a hat, and I realised today that it was because it just about poked out from under the hat. To give it a chance of surviving the walk I contrived a beak from loo roll made into papier-mâché – it was a really good Cyrano de Bergerac conk. After all, I thought, the nose should really arrive at the destination marginally before the rest of me – unless I walked backwards on the last stage, and I wasn't going to do that and let the damned rucksack get there first. It didn't deserve to complete the trip at all, and I almost said so aloud so it'd hear.

The false nose poking out under the brim of my hat caused great mirth among passers-by, and I was rewarded with several toots from passing cars. Leaving Arrens I made a risky decision and bought five Mars bars hoping they would not melt before I could eat them. I also bought another phone card at a tabac and hoped it would work – I seemed to be having some sort of trouble with phones.

This phone issue was going to get a lot worse.

Part of the route was through an arboretum with very easy paths, and comfortable walking conditions. I stopped frequently to read name tags on trees, all of which I found I'd forgotten by the time I wrote up the day's log.

The last part on the road was very hot and I avoided some of the GR10 detours off the road for the sake of the knee – le genou – and so I kept to the old GR10 along the road. Old *ballises* were still visible, even though attempts had been made to remove them.

The Hôtel Lac d'Estaing.

I decided to cosset myself again and booked in here for the night. A sultry waitress sauntered over to where I'd seated myself at a table and asked if I wanted the midday meal.

"No thanks," I said, stretching, "I'm just resting after a very long walk, and I don't eat at midday."

She looked a little surprised – I think she looked at a clock on the far wall as a way of emphasising that it was rather early in the day to have completed *a very long walk*. Well, she didn't know I hadn't been walking all night.

Anyway, she had just turned to go back to wherever waitresses go, when I added, "Oh, OK, I'll just have a coffee please," – as if I was doing them a favour. I should have seen what was coming, because a few minutes after the coffee I had a beer, and about fifteen minutes after that – totally surprised and with the smiling waitress looking benevolently on – I found myself ploughing through the Plat du jour. It consisted of a good salad, faux filet, myrtilles and fromage blanc again, and, naturally, a pichet of red wine – again. I honestly don't know how it happened and can only plead diminished responsibility.

Feeling physically content, but mentally wretched at my continuing unbridled gluttony, I idly kicked some stones and beat a few nettles as I strolled by the lake, and eventually sunbathed and watched a kite festival in the distance. A few hundred yards or so down the lake some fliers were using the kites to pull them on a ski / snowboard type of float.

Lying on the grass, I was amused (sent into hysterics is more accurate) to watch a small man in half a uniform with a whistle stuck in his mouth. He wore dark blue trousers held up by braces, a grubby white shirt (half untucked), and a colour-coordinated dark blue peaked cap with a white mark on the front that could have been a badge, or a well-aimed hit from a seagull. His source of authority was not obvious, but he clearly thought he was *it*. There were some bright orange traffic cones to constrict traffic for no obvious reason, and this non-commissioned dictator was in charge of them, and therefore in charge of the entire flow of the considerable volume of motorised visitors.

There were no traffic lights or other visual controls, and everything was done by sound and a frantic wind-milling of the arms. Nothing was left to the free will of the motorist, and even if there was no traffic from one direction, any attempt to get past the cones was repelled with unbelievable ferocity and loud short blasts from the whistle that he had somehow set to automatic fire. With his chin jutting forward, he simultaneously raised and waved both arms as if he was shaking dust from an invisible Persian rug. When he'd stopped one incursion, he'd whirl round to make sure there was no attempt to get past from the other direction. After he'd established that there was no traffic flow at all, he'd choose one side, square up to it, and then the wind-milling started. With another withering blast from the whistle, the arms flew as if he was swimming backstroke, and since the stretch of cones was only about fifteen yards, he could skull up and down his territory like a demented water-beetle, defending it and the cones as the need arose.

There seemed no point whatsoever to this, and I'd just begun to suspect that the cones were his personal property, and that he was rehearsing an act for some sort of dramatic fringe festival, when an ice-cream van arrived. He promptly heaved a few cones to one side, the ice-cream van took up its clearly reserved spot, and the jingle started. Time to move on I thought, as I discovered my right hand in my pocket, stealthily rummaging through the loose change.

Tomorrow I shall keep to the road wherever possible and use the knee bandage – I might even cut the back out of the bandage if necessary to stop it chaffing behind the knee.

There are several climbs and descents tomorrow – no worse than the dreaded Hourquette d'Arre, given that I'm starting from the lac instead of Arrens. Castle says six and a half hours – I'll give it ten – start 07:00 easy! That's the sort of mental reassurance that I would invent from time to time. The waitress snared me again in the evening with a bait of Cassoulet au Confit d'Oie (goose) – excellent. Bed at 20:25.

Day 23: Lac d'Estaing to Cauterets
07:00 – 15:35

I started well with the knee bandage on, and although it was sunny, I was in the shade of the mountains early on. I got to the Col d'Ilhéou in Castle's recommended time – fantastic, after three weeks I am now an average rambler. I would not have imagined that was possible back in the foothills. It was wonderfully cool and shady till just before the Col. Then it became sunny, not too hot – but the difference is immediately noticeable. I didn't touch the water till that point. This is the way to do it – I actually enjoyed the ascent stage to the Col. Was it the cool, the Col, or the Cassoulet d'Oie perhaps? or maybe it was yesterday's sunbathing rest, or maybe a combination of all of those.

I had a bit of trouble finding the route to bypass the Refuge d'Ilhéou – I suddenly came across a broken fence and a serious cliff edge – this was not the right way at all, and it would have been very nasty in mist. This happened after I'd intentionally gone against the *ballises* because I thought their direction and trend looked wrong, and I suspected either a detour, or that I'd skipped a section somewhere without realising it, and that I was pointing back to Hendaye.

It was my position estimate that was wrong. I found I was disoriented and going round in circles. To get to the earlier cliff edge I'd even gone against a GR10 X negation marker. I sat for a while, got myself in hand, and retraced my steps to a point where I could see the refuge. This was at about 2073 metres altitude, and there was indeed a branch in the GR10.

In spite of the self-administered warning I got during the preceding hour, I eventually got lower down, and onto the Gave d'Ilhéou that led east and northeast to Cauterets, by careful contouring and common sense rather than by following way markers. This was one of the rare times when the *ballises* were visible but seemed difficult or not necessary to follow.

There was now a terribly long descent on a stony track, and I had to take it at a very slow pace – because of my left knee. I had many agonising lock-ups when, instead of the left knee bending as the right foot went forward, the left knee seemed to lock straight and catapult me upwards and forwards instead. This was very unpleasant when the track was descending. The problem didn't occur in the same way when going up. I almost fell many times and was eventually reduced to less than a snail's pace. Later, during a steep descent through woods and over some large rocks it was even worse, and as I finally entered Cauterets I was quite literally sweating with the pain. At this moment I expected the expedition was finished, not because I didn't want to go on, or couldn't manage the pain, but because I simply could not walk.

It had become misty, grey, cold – not raining exactly, but the mist was visibly and densely falling and saturating everything. This was not what I'd planned or begun to experience earlier that day, and it was characteristic of the changes of fortune which can occur in a very short time.

I eventually found and checked in at the gîte d'étape – Le Pas de l'Ours.

I took the name to mean either *the way of the bear*, or *the bear's footprint or footstep* – maybe it was intended to be all of those things, a French pun. Whatever its translation, it was up a side street behind a Lôgis de France of the same name. It took me something like an hour to cross about a quarter of a mile of Cauterets, and to climb the hill to the gîte.

Many small hotels and Lôgis have a down-market gîte attached for walkers, and I certainly felt down-market.

I had the whole place to myself – there was no-one else there.

Dinner was my own concoction – a minestrone / pasta / three egg saucepan-full of delight – plus chilli powder of course. It was far too much, but I forced it down. I then saw off a pint or so of pamplemousse (grapefruit) juice, and a yoghurt.

Unbelievably I could walk again. I could only put it down to the food – I took no medication.

I bought a cheap fleece – a light coloured one, and immediately got minestrone flecks on it when I had seconds in order to reinforce the knee repair. Slept like a log again.

Day 24: Rest at Cauterets

I wrote up the log at the Place Fôch over a coffee.

There were no cordoniers (boot menders) in town, but I bought a tube of neoprene contact glue, and a new toothbrush – I could use the old broken one to clean the boot for gluing – smart eh!

10:05 some blue sky was now visible – what a difference to the spirits.

It's my friend Clive's 60th birthday – I decided that I must phone him later. It was the 6th day of the 6th month and he was 60 – that could be interpreted as 666 the mark of the beast. I must tell him, I thought, he would like that.

Cauterets has a good range of sport shops and there was an excellent pair of lightweight very supportive Meindl boots for sale at a reasonable price – I was very tempted. Overall it's very touristy here, but still quite attractive. I bought lip and nose sun block, and I also considered making another substantial beak with the left-over neoprene glue, but then rejected it on the basis that it might turn out to be permanent. It was a shame really, I could have made a really impressive beak with all that glue, and I could have added a handful of pigeon feathers for good effect.

I flushed the boot cavity using only water, and scrubbed it clean. I then left it for about forty five minutes in hot sun so that it would dry. A year later I can still smell the vibram sole frying in the sun. If the glue failed I decided that I would buy the Meindl boots in the town centre, and send the failed Scarpa boots back.

It was while I spent this day at Cauterets that my wife Lesley obtained the generous offer from Cotswold Camping to send out a replacement pair of boots – IF – I sent back the damaged pair. I had no idea in what footwear I was expected to walk, during what would have been a two week turnaround time.

I glued the boots at the expense of two spoons, an old kitchen knife, and two pens, all of which I used as spreaders and spacers. I would have to see if I had to pay for them. Oh, plus a broken toothbrush of course. Later on the boot looked solid enough, but only walking would tell.

Berlingôt fabrication seems to be the main industry of the area. These are tetrahedral shaped sweets of all flavours and colours. Thermal baths, and a general tourist base are the other main offerings of Cauterets.

I tried to visit the thermal baths but they didn't open until 18th June, and when I read the list of treatments I reckoned that it was probably just as well. These included delights such as: Gargarismes (whatever they are I don't want to meet one), Collective Inhalation (if everyone did it together we could end up in a vacuum), and Pulverisation for goodness sake.

I started to make notes about my daughter Erika's arrival, and gave myself a liberal portion of pasta, egg, and chorizo. And chilli of course. Bed at 22:00.

Day 25: Cauterets to Luz-Saint-Sauveur
07:30 – 16:00

I made a good early start and it was a shady, mostly easy walk to the Col de Riou. On the way a herd of sheep surrounded me inquisitively, and they nibbled my rucksack, straps, trousers, even the batons Anglais. They seemed intent on trying anything different to the boring pasture. They really were a crowd of comedians – or rather comediennes.

I actually beat the posted time. It was an easy zigzag on good tracks – and I thought that perhaps the time / pace setter had a bad day.

After descending from the Col de Riou to the now snow-less ski lift base area I saw a couple, in their early sixties I should guess, arrive by car. The man asked me what the view was like from *up there* – pointing to the top of the Col as if he was waving a sword at it to keep it at bay. His wife was fidgeting as if she needed the loo. I said it was very *jolie*, and that you could see Cauterets. They thought about this, and then, in a squeaky voice that had the same effect on me as sucking a lemon, his wife asked if they could drive up there. I replied that I'd seen a service van at the top of the track, and that it might make a reasonable adventure for them. Looking me closely in the eye the man then said very slowly something to the effect of ...*so, ... you ... can ... see ... Cauterets?*

Now, at this point I thought they were trying to catch me out, so I made a show of thinking about my answer, and said just as slowly, while making a (respectable) two-fingered walking motion, *"...yes, ... I've ... just ... walked... from ... there."*

I'd hardly finished the last syllable when they looked up the hill behind me, rolled their eyes in horror, and rushed to their car and started the engine.

I couldn't imagine what I'd done, and so I suddenly imagined – I can't help it at times – that they'd seen something – a bear maybe – behind me.

I therefore now lurched quickly after them hastily looking over my shoulder, and ready to fling myself onto the roof of the car if necessary. I can be pretty good at getting out of tight spots, but at this instant I think they thought I was chasing them, because the lady gave a sort of stifled squeal and I heard the central locking mechanism of the car. That was the second time this trip that I'd been seen as some sort of monster and had provoked such defensive action. *What's wrong with me?* I thought miserably, *my face isn't green and I don't have a bolt sticking out of my neck.* I hastily felt it to make sure.

She might just have sneezed I thought, trying to mitigate the self-doubt, but at that instant, presumably as a result of my rush towards them, it seemed that the driver was spurred into a renewed frenzy to escape, and they shot away with the wheels spinning, and showering me with pebbles as I shielded my face and stood watching them with my mouth open. The whole incident only lasted about two or three minutes. They were clearly as mad as a couple of hatters.

Not long after this farce I had the honour to encounter a man who was maintaining the *ballises* with red and white paint – some were actually still wet – and after chatting with him and assuring him how much his work was appreciated, I took a photograph of him at work from a distance. The photograph tells me it was the 7th June at 10:32.

There were some very pleasant stretches on the way to a place called Grust – beautiful flower meadows, a very ancient bridge, and fairly widespread use of large flat stones as fencing – reminiscent of the type that I'd seen in old Celtic parts of Mayenne and Normandy much further north.

There was a truly wonderful and memorable shady walk, and at the time I felt elated and that it was a high point in the whole trip. This grassy, tree-lined avenue led to what seemed to me to be a very special hazel wood. There was evidence of long abandoned coppicing, and the area was scattered with huge boulders that made me feel their positions weren't entirely random – maybe it was a relatively recently overgrown ancient megalithic pagan site. There are such things I told myself hopefully.

As I poked about in the undergrowth I could see that the whole area was criss-crossed by long-established trackways, and it certainly had a very ancient feel to it; parts of the woodland made me think of sacred groves. There was nothing sinister about it at all, and I was really enjoying the day.

Then everything went, as they say, pear-shaped.

First of all I noticed that the boot-gluing was a total failure, and that the left sole was now completely detached in the centre – it was held on fore and aft only.

Next, in order to get to Luz, I tried to take a shortcut at a place called Sazos that was near another place called Sassis. Between them I got totally muddled, and I ended up skulking across some private land to reach the road. What a road. Heat and more heat. Kilometre after kilometre of hot exhausting trek to Luz-Saint-Sauveur. I've heard the Ariège is hot – if it's anything like this it'll be murder. My road route was actually parallel with the GR10 that passed through trees at a slightly higher altitude, and I would most certainly have been better off sticking to it.

I visited a couple of boot shops – I desperately wanted the Meindl boots from Cauterets – but I couldn't find anything similar at Luz. I even looked at the map and considered taking a taxi back to Cauterets to get them, but it was too far by road. There was a large *Intersport* shop with a good selection of other lighter and cheaper, fairly good-looking trekking boots.

I booked into the Hôtel de Londres, showered, shaved, and I was sitting in the Place du 8 Mai (that was about a week before I started I thought) with a large Heineken pression (draught). It said 17:14 on the multi-function wrist-beast, my good old analogue watch was full of condensation again. *Intersport* were open till 19:00 so there was plenty of time to get ratted and go and taunt the shoe sales people.

I eventually settled for new boots – size ten and a half instead of ten, after much mulling. They were made by a company called Millet, and this made me think of the long-established firm of Millets back in Britain, and from whom I bought my hat in far off Yeovil, Somerset. I assumed there was no connection between the companies.

Intersport were very helpful – they packaged up the offending Scarpa boots, and even offered to take them to the post for me at no extra charge. Unfortunately the post-office had already closed.

Dinner at the Hôtel de Londres watching wild trout swimming in the river – it sounded rather grand.

Salade gourmande, tournedos (poivre vert) – sadly it wasn't saignant (rare) like I asked, but it was still very good and not worth a complaint. I'm English and put up with anything. I ended up having two half bottles of cuvée de la maison because I'd tried to be good and have just one half bottle, but, failing to synchronise with the fromage, I simply had to have a second. It was just as well I started with only a half bottle – that steak was really good and just begged for as much wine accompaniment as possible. Two armagnacs (sheep as for a lamb I thought), and a couple of coffees.

Fabulous ambience after an awful latter part of the day.

I can't start early tomorrow because I need to wait for the post to open. The Scarpa boots have been a very bad negative influence ever since the plateau de Lhers, and I shall be glad to see the back of them. They'd looked great, but under the conditions for which they were supposedly designed they turned out to be utter rubbish. Expensive rubbish.

Selected Photographs Béarn

Day 16 – 29 May 14:31
The descent to Borce – what goes down has to go up.

Day 17 – 30 May 09:32
The Chemin de la Mature with the Fort Du Portalet beyond.

Day 17 – 30 May 14:38
The way forward to the Col de la Hourquette de Larry at 2055 metres.
This was 5 hours after the previous photo, and the day had started at 08:00.

Day 17 – 30 May 17:22
The Pic du Midi d'Ossau from the Col d'Ayous at 2200 metres.
No ballise visible, so which is the way to go – keeping the Pic du Midi
d'Ossau on the right?

Day 17 – 30 May 17:22
Or – keeping the Pic du Midi d'Ossau on the left?
A mistake might be fatal.

Day 18 – 31 May 06:49
Made the right choice last night – this was the view next morning over Lac
Gentau at 1947 metres.

Day 18 – 31 May 07:42
Looking back at the Refuge D'Ayous from the other side of Lac Gentau.

Day 19 – 01 June 11:29
Looking back down towards Gabas after four and a half hours. The village
is somewhere beyond the forests in the centre.

Day 19 – 01 June 16:32
Again, looking back towards the day's start. It's nine and a half hours after
beginning, and I'm now several miles beyond the point of no return. Hard
to believe I was the other side of the Pic du Midi d'Ossau, left in the photo,
only a couple of days previously.

Day 19 – 01 June 16:32
The way forwards, up towards the nightmare of the Hourquette d'Arre at 2465 metres. Sadly, the dangers of the rest of this day proved too formidable for photography, and I didn't realise at this point that I was going to slither, roll, fall and curse a vertical 400 metres to get to the night's bivouac stop.

Day 20 – 02 June 07:53
A frozen Lac d'Anglas the next morning at 2070 metres. My bivvy bag, rucksack, poles, boots and water bottle are on the raised ground in the centre. The other tents were those of fishermen from Gourette, away and down to the right.

Day 21 – 03 June 11:12
Gourette had been left behind and the D918 was somewhere below.

Day 21 – 03 June 12:40
On the D918, crossing the first Pyrénéan divide.

Day 23 – 05 June 08:17
The way forward, and the sun still wasn't up.

Day 23 – 05 June 11:53
Nearly midday, very hot, and about to descend towards the Refuge d'Ilhéou by the lake, and take the nightmare Gave d'Ilhéou heading down to the left.

Day 25 – 07 June 13:03
One of the ancient boulder-strewn trackways around Grust.

6   Bigorre, Hautes-Pyrénées, Haute-Garonne
Day 26: Luz-Saint-Sauveur to Barèges
10:30 – 12:30

It was monster hot and too late, I thought, to take the lengthy off-road GR10 so I took the road route. It was another form of nightmare. Uphill, little or no shade, and constant traffic – never do it again. If it's too late to leave in hot weather (after 07:30) then it would be better to wait for the next day if necessary, rather than to choose a road connection. In my case at this point, given that the timescale fitted, I should have done just that. I decided I needed to find out more about the nature of future stages in advance, and to maybe start at dawn.

I arrived at Barèges as a dehydrated husk.

The village was a sort of slit in the countryside with nothing at all to commend it. I made my way to the Hôtel de la Poste and checked in to what was a very old-fashioned, quaint little place, full of elderly and sedate people moving about very slowly. On closer inspection I expected to see that they were festooned with cobwebs, but mercifully there was only the odd money spider and gnat.

I'd just stepped outside to reassure myself that I was still alive, when a middle-aged couple in a car stopped to ask me if they were going the right way for the Cirque de Gavarnie, an impressive curtain of vertical mountainside that encircles the head of a nearby valley. I showed them on their map where they were – the middle of tiny Barèges, where any idiot should have been able to orient himself – and that they were not going the right way. They turned the car in a parking area opposite where I stood, and I clearly saw the lady actually turning the map upside down so that she could then presumably look along the road on the map in the same direction that the car was pointing. Of course she couldn't then read the town names so easily and, when she twisted in the seat so as to keep the map pointing the right way, she'd get a stiff neck, lose where she was on the map, and they'd have to stop and find someone else to tell them where they were. I imagined them later on, travelling along the zigzag roads with hair-pin bends, him wrenching the steering wheel through three hundred and sixty degrees, and her flapping and rotating the map until again they hadn't a clue where they were.

Ham, omelette and chips – bed.

Day 27: Barèges to Cabin at Lac d'Aubert
07:00 – 16:00

It rained all night. I looked out at 06:25 and saw that it was misty and drizzling, and dived back under the covers. At 06:45 everything looked clear and I thought great, let's get out there and conquer.

After the usual morning ablutions there was even worse mist at 07:00 – only fifty metres visibility. This was a devastating blow to the high spirits of only a quarter of an hour ago. It just showed how quickly the weather can vary in the mountains.

After breakfasting in the room from a tray I *forced* myself out – hoping it would clear later and higher. In these circumstances there's no-one to rely on for a boost or a threat to get you moving, you just *do or falter*.

I had to make a difficult decision when the time came to leave the road and strike out over the mountains. It was still drizzling and there was a heavy mist. I stood on the road a couple of miles or so outside Barèges and looked around despondently. This was a really depressing environment. I'd hated the road walking the day before. I knew that if I waited around for the weather to clear that it might then be too late to avoid another frying. From where I was there was no real safe or road route that I could take in bad weather anyway – the route unavoidably went up into the mountains – away from nasty old civilisation. I took a BIG gamble here, and just thought damn it I'm going. I assured myself I'd take extreme care, I'd rigidly keep to the track, and if there was a problem, then I'd get in the sack (bivvy not ruck), and wait it out.

I'd got plenty of good rations for about three days so I was bullet-proof.

1500 feet higher and two hours later it was still grim but *maybe* there was just a hint of a lighter shade of sky ahead – i.e. further up. It did clear locally after a while, but the distant snow-covered mountains were still partially obscured by low cloud.

Around lunchtime – ten o'clock! – the clouds dispersed and I found myself in a wide sheltered valley; under milky blue skies, and beside a clear shallow stream with a fine gravel bed. The stream came towards me from the distant Col de Madamète. The valley sides swept upwards gracefully, and they were decorated with broken rock that looked like it had been dispensed from a celestial pepper mill. Throughout this stone-spattered landscape there were stunted pines, and large tracts of vertically-challenged spiky grass. It was a stunning mixture of windswept desolation and great beauty – but then that's the nature of most of the Pyrénées.

To the gentle murmuring of the stream I sat down and had lunch. Stale, stretchy bread, sardines, some sweaty cheese, and a peach that I'd taken great care to prevent from bruising. It was a sumptuous banquet in the circumstances, and I sat and smiled inanely at the inanimate objects around me that so often conspired to cause me grief. A temporary armistice had been declared in this alpine paradise – unimaginable three hours earlier.

The stream, I'd noticed earlier, terminated against a mountainous slope of disordered fallen rock that was quite oblique to the direction of fall of the valley. The rock fall was like a barricade, and the stream just went up to it and disappeared. There was no obvious pothole, the stream simply met the impenetrable wall – and then went through it. There must once have been a second valley that had been blocked off by some catastrophic geological event in a bygone era. I stood and watched, fascinated, as thousands of gallons of water an hour – every hour – just vanished from this world into another dimension.

Just as I finished my lunch I noticed a berger and his dog driving a flock of delinquent sheep up the valley about fifty metres the other side of the stream. He must have a hut somewhere, I thought, since we were many miles from a road.

Some of the sheep were particularly recalcitrant, and one of these left the main body and passed behind me on some sort of mission to distract and taunt the dog. I got the impression that it was doing it for a dare. The berger spotted this, and as he looked in my direction we exchanged nods. The next moment he issued some command to the dog, and seemed to point at me. Now this dog was very focussed on his task, and as he rushed towards me I thought for a moment that the shepherd was trying to round *me* up. I took up a defensive pole posture, but the dog rushed past almost brushing me with his tail but without the slightest acknowledgement of my presence. With the dog in hot pursuit the lone sheep took off up the hillside and incredibly seemed to lose the dog among the tumbled rocks. I imagined cheers from the distant flock at such unlikely ovine audacity and derring-do.

Minutes later the dog appeared on top of a prominent rock and, looking back at the berger, whined anxiously. The berger whistled some code and pointed, and the dog leapt off in another direction, only to emerge on top of another rock with the same appeal for another clue.

This went on for some time with the dog getting more upset, and with the berger becoming more and more annoyed until he finally slapped his forehead with the flat of his hand, shouted some incomprehensible French, and turned his back. This was more than the dog could handle, and the poor thing howled as if he'd received a physical rebuke and charged after his boss. I missed their reunion and whatever punishment or commiseration took place because they disappeared after the main flock which had fanned out as if at some anti-berger-like command from within their own ranks. They'd all charged off into a more substantial pine wood lower down the valley and the berger was now in hot pursuit.

Turning to look back in the direction of the dog's fruitless search I could just make out a furtive white face peeping out from a small thicket. I have no doubt it was smiling and, having won the contest, the plucky escapee trotted out after a sufficient delay and went off after the others – no doubt to exchange notes on dog dodging over a few mouthfuls of stunted grass and a slurp or two of the bubbling local stream water.

For me the Col de Madamète was almost another Hourquette d'Arre.

I couldn't find the trail at one point, so I took a route that I thought looked *nicer* – for goodness sake. What was I coming to? Stop and look around *really* carefully. Do some careful compass work. It does work if you take the time. The real trail surely had to be over to the right and beyond another ridge – not the *nice* one. The compass agreed that over to the right was more likely to be the way to go, so off I went.

I'd got it – I found a *ballise* and I was as happy as if I'd found an exposed seam of gold; but what a route – there were more snow fields, HUGE boulders to climb over – slip between them and you would never be seen again. I wondered about going back and taking the *nice* route – wherever it led.

One of the phenomena to be seen at this time of the year and at this altitude in the mountains is worthy of a little description. The snow is still mostly continuous in large fields, but there are many dark rocks sticking up out of it like islands in a frozen sea of ice. These inviting islands, sometimes covered in slicked down grass and looking like a middle-aged head-without-hope, are truly welcome if you can make a landfall without foundering just as you think you're home and dry so to speak. And believe me, the lure of these solid repositories is irresistible after some time of struggling through a quicksand of soft snow.

The difficulty is due (so I calculate) to the warming effect of the sun on the rocks which causes the snow and ice to melt where it's in contact with the rock, and so to recede like the tide, leaving a distasteful and sombre moat of emptiness around the immediate rock. Furthermore, a no-man's-land of unreliable footing spreads out into the snow field for some distance from the rock. Sometimes this is two or three feet or more.

Now, in order to jump from snow field to rock, over the grim moat, it requires a certain amount of extra pressure on the trailing foot to effect a leap which is long enough to reach the rock. This of course causes the spring-boarding foot to sink into the snow resulting in an unseemly sprawling demonstration of the splits – more of a burlesque than a can-can – accompanied by much shouting and snow beating.

It revealed just how thick the snow still was, but how unstable it is at the margin of rocks as the thaw approaches. Sometimes I went through the snow up to my waist. If this happened at the edge of a snowfield then it wasn't too much of a problem because it would just be a small snow-plough impression to reach solid ground. If such a collapse happened in the middle of a vast expanse of snow, then the only remedy was to lie flat, in order to spread the load, and then gradually extract oneself and attempt to get back on two feet by a gradual progression through hands, using the poles to spread the load, via knees, onto four limbs, and then a final cautious act that took primates millions of years to achieve – i.e. to rejoin the ranks of *Homo erectus*.

Many times this evolution would result in an immediate regression to a waist deep posture, accompanied by Neanderthal rantings, and no significant progress whatsoever over the ground.

Frequently with no-one in sight, or even within ten or fifteen miles, and with the thought that no-one knew I was exactly where I was, this could be a little disconcerting and I do not recommend crossing such snow fields without snow shoes – *raquettes* in French.

After such diversions I eventually got to the Col and looked around. Fantastic views. Apart from the berger, now far behind me, I hadn't seen a soul all of that nightmare day – it was great – I actually loved it. Really.

On the Col it started raining and as I went lower I had to pass through more snow and over more boulders by a lake – it was awful I thought, I don't ever want to see anything like this again – not till I'm dry anyway. I hated it. Really.

The first obvious building at lac d'Aubert was all shut up – what to do? – I could bivvy in the rain – not an attractive idea. There were two couples just returning to their car from a pleasant stroll. They were all well-kitted, and possessed the air of the sturdy-looking rambler. I watched them slyly from behind a tree and I wondered if I could get the car keys and be off before they could stop me. I decided not and strolled out into the open and looked pitiful. I tried flattening my ears but it didn't work. I must practice harder. I tried whining and grizzling quietly but they either didn't hear or else they ignored me. As they drove away I imagined the scene back at their hotel or wherever – warm bath, good food, good cuddle – stop it I thought, you're becoming a peeping Pierre or whatever the French equivalent is.

It was from this depth of despair, loneliness, depression, and self-loathing, and any other negative thought that I could conjure up – I was on the point of taking it out on the rucksack for getting me into this mess – that I spotted the second cabin.

It was a little closer to the lake over on the right, and it was separated from where I stood by some rocks and a few stunted trees. The rucksack seemed to relax on my back and we moved towards the cabin fearing the worst – it was probably locked as well.

The stable door top in the entrance to the cabin was open, and inside there were bunks – two continuous levels with a capacity for about six to eight people per level – there were shelves, a long wooden table, and long wooden benches or *forms* as we used to call them at school. There were also two French middle-agers sitting at the table doing nothing that seemed obvious. I suspected that it was some sort of private cabin and asked, without expecting a positive answer, if anyone could use it. They looked a little disappointed.

"Oui," they both replied simply .

"Oh merci, merci beaucoup," I slobbered, and I bagged a spot suitably away from their position, though there wasn't a lot of room for manoeuvre. After a minor exchange of pleasantries it became obvious that they were not at all open to conversation. Fair enough, there's nothing worse than having some speaking donkey imposed upon you, especially in a confined space.

So, we were all sitting there writing logbooks or doing cross-words when two Spanish skiers arrived with a box full of food – they'd obviously got a car as well. A little while later another Spanish couple arrived with another box of food. Was this a shrine I wondered – some pilgrim's hideaway perhaps? They sat for five minutes in a huddled talk, and then left. Maybe my socks had caught something from Klaus's. They took the box of food as well damn it.

I looked at my maps, logbook, and notes for the next few days. There was now no leeway on me getting to Fos for the next Saturday as I'd planned, unless I could get to Vielle-Aure tomorrow. I decided on a very early start, and, weather permitting, I might then just make it. On chatting a bit more with the French couple – I think I let them start it – they said that le meteo (the weather forecast) warned of an orage (a storm) for tomorrow – that's just great.

It's a good job I've staked my claim to a bunk – another group has just arrived – all laughing middle-aged ladies – so it looks like we're going to have a party. This group of three corpulent ladies had great fun getting onto the top bunk. The *ladder* was a pole with short staggered branches sticking out each side. Thankfully it was well-anchored. One large femme kept going up this contraption to the top where she would lift a leg, change position, lift the other leg, and then tut and grunt. She failed each time to make the transition into the bunk, and then she came down again to howls of laughter from the other two. And from the rest of us. The view from below was of an enormous tethered hot-air balloon with a couple of short legs, gracelessly going up and down a pole, and shuddering at each change of direction. This happened a few times and then they developed a variant. One of the three stayed on the floor making sympathetic noises and giving encouragement, and the third more athletic lady who was already on top, hooted or barked at her just when she almost made it, so that she had hysterics again and slithered back down. This was repeated over and over again. My sides ached, and tears streamed down our faces. I thought it was never going to stop and I wanted to beg for mercy, but I couldn't get the words out in English let alone French. Eventually of course she made it onto the bunk with a gasp and a shriek that brought the house down. There was a standing ovation and calls of *bravo*, and *encore* from everyone. We had just about recovered, and the Femme Française was recumbent on her chosen bunk, looking like a woolly rhinoceros in her fleece.

Just when we thought it was over we were treated again.

"Ou est la toilette?" the woolly rhinoceros asked loudly, and the realisation that we might have to go through the whole thing in reverse was enough to cause a riot.

The capacity for milking a gag isn't just English, I've seen it many times in Europe. When I worked in Antwerp I once saw a dozen Belgian engineers laugh for most of the day at a jug of water that fell over and soaked some documents.

Everything had been peaceful in the cabin for some time, and all were quietly reading or writing. Occasionally, someone would giggle, I guess, at the memory of the assault on the top bunk – my sides were aching for long afterwards. We were all in this relaxed state when we heard a number of people approaching, and a chattering, cavorting group of twenty-five walkers (I counted them) came in carrying boxes, bottles, and cooking utensils. If they were intending to sleep here it was going to get very cosy indeed.

They were there just to cook and eat until dark – what a racket – I was trying to sleep but quite enjoying the commotion in the background. It was very similar to gatherings that we have at home with large groups of friends. I was too knackered to get involved, though I felt I would have been made welcome.

Day 28: Cabin at Lac d'Aubert to Saint-Lary
07:30 – 13:00

As I set off down the trail I passed the party of twenty-five as they set off with ice-picks to do a circular walk after camping by the nearby barrage, or dam. They made a very merry crowd.

The day was made up of fifteen to sixteen miles of lakeside, fell, and a small amount of road walking – all in rain and mist. They were small roads and there was no problem from traffic, but I was quickly soaked right through – my Gore-Tex was old and leaked like a sieve. I needed to make this ground cover to be able to get to Fos for the fifteenth when I was expecting to see Erika.

Overall, the Leki poles were an indispensable ally, but on one occasion they threatened to betray me. I was negotiating a slippery descent over stream-washed pebbles where a water course appeared to have been incorrectly diverted onto the path – or *vice versa*. Without any sort of warning pre-slither, both my feet went forwards from under me and I instinctively put my arms out to minimise the impact. I can only assume that the two Leki poles caught in pebbles behind me and then lodged underneath the rucksack as I slid forwards. The result was that I landed on my back and on top of both poles which were crossed behind and beneath me, and that my wrists were tightly bound by the pole straps to the outstretched pole handles. It was like being crucified. I couldn't move my arms because they were tied to the poles, and I couldn't get off the poles because I was tied to them and they were crossed behind and beneath me.

For several seconds I lay in the stream bed with water coursing into the back of my trousers, my hat over my face, and unable to move. I could have snapped the Leki poles, and was very tempted to do so (that'd teach 'em), but overall they were too useful. The remedy was a violent shouting and bouncing downstream on my back for some metres until the poles emerged behind and above me. I could then sit up, shake off my hat, and shout even louder. I finally climbed out of the stream, soaked from the waist down, furious and gyrating with the poles that had now become a pair of flails. After that I always tried to keep the poles pointing forwards, and my hands inside my own shoulder width on down-hill stretches.

I couldn't find a gîte d'étape, so after I'd checked in at the Hôtel de la Neste at the end of the day I went to my room and found that I'd got so wet and cold that my fingers wouldn't undo the rucksack cover. I had to use both my frozen claws to turn the hot tap on and soak my hands before I could remove the cover and then undo the rucksack. Everything outside the rucksack was totally soaked. The rucksack of course was reposing warm and dry in a corner. I went over and kicked it. My Castle book was saturated, and I sat in the bar with an Armagnac or two for a long time drying the pages individually so they wouldn't stick together. Everything else was laid out on chairs, a spare bed, draped over the television, or dangled from any projection that I could find around the room. It was like a Chinese laundry except that it was all fusty and grubby. For tomorrow le meteo says it will be the same. I wondered if that included all my wet gear, and decided it was up to me.

Although it is a Lôgis de France advertising local specialities, there was no carte, only the repas – the meal of the day. I was told that it was too early in *the season*. The soup was something like cream of cornflour by the look and taste – horrid tasteless. I'd forgotten to bring the chilli powder down again – it might have reincarnated it. I'd originally meant to bring the chilli for the tarte aux poireaux (leek tart). It had sounded insipid to me earlier, but when it arrived it wasn't bad and didn't need spicing up. Pork fingers next, pasta, tomato, cucumber. Chocolate sponge after. It was more than a sponge and with crème anglaise it was very good.

As always, everything was okay after the meal, and thank goodness for a short day tomorrow – unless I try to steal a further march that is. I made a note to remember that although I carried enough food for about three days, and felt comfortable with that, you need *hot* food when you're wet in a cabin – or outside one. I'd sent my cooking gear back home from Saint-Jean-Pied-de-Port. Erika must bring it back out again.

Day 29: Saint-Lary to Germ
09:00 – 18:00

Blue skies were back again and it was hot and sunny.

Le Meteo had got it wrong. It was now too hot and too dry, can't they get anything right? I sunbathed for an hour or so on the Couret de Latuhe – it was very hot at times but there was some shade. For the first time the day ended with an ascent. I knew it would be bad and it was. 400 metres at the end of the day is not good. Loudenvielle – all shut – Mardi (Tuesday) closing of course – common and I should have remembered. I'd wanted some provisions but wasn't going to get them now.

I got to the gîte at Germ and was told by a stand-in – I think he's the cook – *No Vacancies!!* I hung around after persuading him, with some effort, to let me eat there at least. I had the distinct impression he felt I was from the wrong side of the English Channel.

Le patron arrived and quickly found that there was in fact a dormitory for about five with only two in it. What a surprise.

Philippe is one of them, and a very pleasant fellow. He had started at Hendaye on the 1st May and was taking three months. He was also meeting up with various bits of his family at times.

There were also a lot of deaf kids staying there, and they were the source of constant animal noises which echoed around the place as they played – some of them on a playstation. They were a good friendly lot and I set out to entertain them a little.

I always put salt and pepper on my bread while waiting for the meal and so I made a show of it so the kids could see. They thought it was great fun to try it as well, but ended up pulling faces at me when they didn't like it. Some of the supervisors had to tell them off continually they were so mischievous.

Day 30: Germ to Granges d'Astau
08:15 – 15:30

Tuesday. Hot and sunny, but some breeze and shade. I saw an Izard (a type of deer or chamois) running towards me in the woods above Astau. It looked as though it was already nervous, and it snorted when it saw me and changed direction; I think it had been startled / chased by a man and his dog who came into view just afterwards, running downhill at a speed I thought was crazy.

Espingo, with its gorgeous lake, had been my original destination but I decided that another 700 metres ascent, again at the end of the day was out of the question. This now makes it too late to do the journey via Luchon to Fos for Saturday. I decided during the walk today that a much better plan would be to go north to Luchon from Granges d'Astau on Wednesday. That would give me three clear days rest in Luchon before Erika and the Ariège. I needed it. I was again totally knackered and depressed this morning. I hadn't had enough sleep, and my feet were a mess with huge blisters on the backs of my heels after the new boots. I decided that I would look for something lighter in Luchon.

Size ten and a half must have been too big. The Scarpa boots had been size ten, and I'd had no problems – apart from their disintegration. I also needed to waterproof my Gore-Tex – it was soaked like a sponge again. Another friendly dog walked with me part of the way out of Germ, up tracks and between rocky outcrops.

My belief that some of Castle's times are a bit optimistic was confirmed by Philippe who was thinner, younger and fitter than me. Also another French walker I passed said Espingo after Astau was *trés dur!* (very hard). There were more friendly dogs at Astau. I spent some time talking with Philippe at length about our mutual interest in Bordeaux wines and our plans of doing the GR10 alone at the start and end, but in company during the middle stages. We seemed to have a lot in common – he was expecting his son to walk with him for a while as well, and also maybe friends and parents.

I then chatted with two South African / Dutch guys at the bar about deteriorating conditions in South Africa – they both lived in Holland now, and worked in the estate agency or real estate business, selling property throughout Europe – particularly southern France. One of them liked walking, the other couldn't understand why anyone would want to do it. I said I couldn't either, but I was trying to find out. He then tried the Leki poles and immediately wanted a pair so that he too could investigate this crazy walking thing. I added a few lines to the plan for Erika – it seemed likely that we should aim for her to exit in the region of Sentein / Bornac, and then to take a bus or taxi to Saint-Girons. This needed some more planning.

Selected Photographs Bigorre

Day 27 – 09 June 09:42
Good riddance to Barèges and its bad weather – it's back down there in the
mist at top right.

Day 27 – 09 June 09:42
Making good progress, but the way forward is very badly marked and stony.

Day 27 – 09 June 09:55
A brief respite from the stony tracks, but still a long way to go.

Day 27 – 09 June 14:17
Four hours later and the underfoot was more hazardous. (Looking back).

Day 27 – 09 June 15:19
A final glance over the shoulder before heading for the Cabin At Lac d'Aubert.

7   Bagnères-de-Luchon, Haute-Garonne, Ariège
     Day 31: Granges d'Astau to Bagnères-de-Luchon
     08:45 – 11:30

It rained most of last night, but then the day was sunny, and not too hot, which was good for a race to Bagnères-de-Luchon. Although an orage had been forecast for later in the day it didn't happen, and keeping up a fast pace I got there in good time, passing through a small village with the unlikely name of Oo.

In Bagnères-de-Luchon there was an Intersport and various other chaussure (shoe) shops, and a fair choice of boot alternatives. The bustling boulevard with lots of brasseries was a good place to lounge about. Sarah, temporarily without Jim and Dougal, was there too. She told me they'd had various problems – mainly blisters, and Dougal had been to the vet.

Lunchtime – Madiran aperitif, noodly potage, salade aux gésiers (duck's gizzards) – more like gésiers aux salade there was so much gésiers – more than you could shake a pole at. More new boots from Intersport again, and as before they were helpful with packing for the pair of Millet boots that were going home. I chose more modern-looking, lightweight boots this time, size ten, snug fit, vibram soles, and very stiff. (not as stiff as the Meindl). I recall Klaus had Meindl, and he had them so long he'd had them repaired because he swore by them. I'd tried on a pair of Meindl boots when I first bought the Scarpa boots, and I thought they were *too* stiff at the time. I have a different view now I've walked a few miles over tough terrain.

I posted the Millet boots home, they certainly weren't in disgrace, and with more time to select an insert, and with less critical breaking in, they would do fine in the future.

Dinner at the Hôtel Bon Acceuil, pretty close to the centre of town, and right next to a large church – potage, entrecôte and purée vegetables – very good – fromage, glâce pruneaux (plum ice-cream).

I'd managed to arrange a deal for a few days, and for a room for Erika when she arrives. The balcony, which faced the church and not the main street, turned out to be good for drying small, unobtrusive bits of washing.

Bagnères-de-Luchon, Haute-Garonne, Ariège

Hôtels don't seem to like their residents festooning the main frontage above reception.

A very loud set of clock / church bells are fortunately stopped at night. They sound the hour twice – once just before, and then again on the hour. I understood that the first announcement was to get your attention if you were out working in the fields for instance, and that the second set of chimes indicated the hour when you were ready for it and prepared to start counting.

Day 32: Rest at Bagnères-de-Luchon

I proofed my Gore-Tex wet wear and the new boots, and then had a horror story trying to get a response, let alone a solution, to problems with my phone card, and to complain about the wastage of my credit because of unreliable French phone boxes.

France Télécom télècabins seemed to me to be unreliable – with random success even in the same box – especially with lengthy international numbers. The charge would be taken from the card even when there was no connection – not no answer – but when their infrastructure failed!

I wondered if code-based cards might be more reliable than chip-based ones, whether it was a timing problem, and if I could get some equipment to run some tests. I could bring a team of friends over from home, and we could solve the problem and also have a great time in Bagnères-de-Luchon getting to the bottom of it. We'd save France Télécom thousands, and still turn in a good profit ourselves. What I didn't realise at the time, of course, was that someone was probably already doing very nicely out of their clients' losses – my losses among them.

I phoned the equivalent of operator services but the unhelpful French operators wouldn't give me any help, and would even cut the line while I tried to explain. They seemed to have no idea of what a service industry should be like. My Francophile tendencies were being drawn out thinner than an optic fibre.

Eventually, after four or five attempts, I got one to listen. She was genuinely pleasant and helpful at first, although, as it turned out, there was still no real solution. She kept saying what sounded like *distress*, and that it was local and the same everywhere. This seemed like a fair philosophical point, but I couldn't see how it helped me. I would then say something, in French of course, to try and get an actual phone *number*.

"Thankyou, yes, I agree that it is *distressing*, everywhere, but who do I contact?"

This circular, apparently one-sided conversation that we were both having was finally resolved when I broke the loop and said very slowly and firmly.

"But – what – is – the – *number* – for – this – *distress* department?"

I thought I heard her catch her breath at this boldness, and in the brief silence the atmosphere between us – two entities invisible to each other – was electric. I could feel her groping across the electronic space between us to strangle me. It reminded me of something from a Stephen King novel.

After a moment's unnerving silence she replied equally slowly and firmly. I knew at this point that she'd taken as much as she could, but that unlike the other mesdames, she couldn't cut me off because we were now in it together – a bit like a hostage situation.

"Dix", she said followed by a long pause, "treize," another pause, "Monsieur."

There was now another long pause during which I was beginning to think she'd fainted from the excitement.

"Dix-treize," she suddenly popped out.

That means *ten-thirteen* if you didn't already know it, and for the first time I heard it as a number not a word.

In French, it sounds like *deece treeers*, and to me, it had previously sounded suspiciously like *distress*, and I'd thought all along that they were being mischievous and taunting me by keeping the number a secret.

She did the *Dix* pause *treize* bit several times, with the pause getting shorter and shorter so it sounded like a steam train slowly accelerating away from a station. At last, as the penny or franc dropped, so to speak, and with the realisation of my error, I was enthralled, captivated. Now I understood everything. As she puffed out each word, I was going up onto the balls of my feet, and then down again. I wanted to join in. We could have sung it as a duet I thought, but I was worried that in so doing, I might have pushed her over the edge if she wasn't already over it.

This was now my chance though, to get my own back for all those times I've said things in French that have not been understood, only to have them eventually repeated back by the French listener, with exactly the same inflection, as if to say *why didn't you say that in the first place?*

In the event I couldn't be too unkind so I just spoke with my best Gallic accent.

"*Aaaah*, Dix-treize, je comprends maintenant – merci trés bien madame, rappellez moi si vous avez la même problème encore," and put the phone down.

I'd said, that I now understood, thanked her, and told her to call me if she had the same problem again.

I could hear a distant police siren getting closer, and I decided to use another box next time since they had obviously already managed to trace the call and would be lying in wait for me. I made several deliberate, false turns as I returned to the hotel to make sure I wasn't being followed. At one point during this diversionary tactic I was followed by a suspicious figure in a long black leather coat and a brown felt hat – clearly Gestapo.

I went back to La Poste and sent another eight hundred grams back home in one of their attractive yellow and blue cardboard boxes – redundant maps, detachable trouser legs, and a few other odds and ends that the rucksack didn't seem to need. I decided my waterproof over trousers would do as a spare long set.

Salade verte, confit de canard and frites at midday – cheap and excellent. There was a minor embarrassment when I went to the loo in the brasserie and found that I'd been swaggering around like a healthy mountain walker for half the day with my trouser zip undone. Unlike some trousers that have a discreet fly, the walking trousers have an inclination to bare their teeth in a huge grin. Maybe it's due to age or to the stress caused by relaxing in the mountains I thought. I looked for an alternative exit to avoid having to pass back through the crowded restaurant, but the window was barred. I was convinced the whole restaurant was ready for me, but they all seemed too polite to comment, and I seemed to get away with just the occasional snigger.

Resealable gas cartridges were surprisingly difficult to find in Bagnères-de-Luchon. Other types were plentiful, but not screw-on, and Erika was bringing the gas burner back to the trail, but she couldn't bring a gas cartridge on the plane of course. I finally got one, so the shopping list I'd made earlier could now be closed and I could have another beer with Philippe who I met by chance outside the Casino shop. This was the same place I'd come across Sarah (without Jim and Dougal) yesterday.

Philippe and I had a couple of beers and discussed the next stages of the GR10 – he was going to Spain to bypass most of the Ariège and he planned to then re-emerge into the Pyrénées-Orientales where he'd booked a week in a French Ministry hostel of some sort. He worked for the French government in civil construction about ten kilometres from Aix-en-Provence.

I noticed that he had some good-looking honey in a plastic container, and so I re-opened the shopping list. I can thoroughly recommend it to any traveller.

He also had a newspaper that forecast another orage for the next few days – that was a very bad idea.

Day 33: Rest at Bagnères-de-Luchon

Erika was arriving today, well, early tomorrow anyway. Bagnères-de-Luchon was very pleasant, the Pyrénées were very pleasant, but I wished she was coming by car so we could get back home and I could do something less hazardous and tiring. Sit in the garden perhaps. I've had more than enough of this – every morning usually starts with a feeling of anxiety / terror. I was free of it yesterday, but had another glimpse of it today because it's back to walking / climbing / dying multiple times again tomorrow. There was presently a blue sky, and it was sunny, with a few fast-moving cumulus clouds at some fifteen to twenty thousand feet. At 09:20 the atmospheric pressure was 938 mBar – it dropped about twelve hours ago, but there was no change during the last six hours. My wrist machine tells me all this and a lot more. I can accurately monitor atmospherics since I'm at a fixed altitude for the day. I should really have calibrated it, and started recording yesterday.

Suddenly, obsessed with technology, I went out and bought a one hundred minute code-based phone card – a unique tariff of FFr 100 – and I tested it on my home number. It seemed okay, and I considered buying another as well because FT agencies are not that widespread. This type of card is specifically aimed at international use, but only from landlines, not for use with a mobile. There is also a free phone information number printed on it – I could, at no charge, become a phone pest.

It seems that biting flies are prolific even during the day. The Pyrénées are full of them. Bedrooms, restaurants, boulevard cafés, shoe shops, FT Télècabins – they'll follow a victim anywhere. I swear one deliberately caused me to knock a glass of wine over when I lashed out at it (at the fly that is).

13:50 Saw Philippe again – same place – the Casino food shop – with his son and coupaine – girlfriend. I think that like Piccadilly, the whole world passes that Casino shop at some time. We talked about Gypaètes, a vulture variant that eats bones as ninety percent of its diet. It drops them from a great height onto rocks so that they break into digestible pieces. Philippe reckoned he'd seen one near Espingo, and that they're quite rare.

17:00 Almost complete, mostly grey, cloud cover. 939 mBar. No significant change over the last six to twelve hours – will it pass by tomorrow morning? I bought some restorative chocolate drinks, Orangina, and snack food for Erika's early morning arrival, just in case she was peckish, and also ordered a flask of tea.

With nothing better to do, I recorded the following meteorological observations while waiting for the small hours to arrive, and rather than throw them away, I present them below. They made incredibly boring reading then, and they haven't really improved over time:

18:20 939 mBar, total grey, no cloud movement, rain, thunder.

21:20 940 mBar, couple of lighter patches – but hail forecast. Distant thunder.

21:42 947 mBar – things might be looking up.

Day 34: Rest at Bagnères-de-Luchon

Erika finally arrived at Bagnères-de-Luchon at 02:11. The plane was late, the train was late, British Airways had lost her luggage, and then were not very helpful. That airline had already tried to tell her the flight was overbooked before she left Britain and so prevent her from coming at all.

Now Erika can be a bit of a tiger when she's roused, and, after receiving some completely un-business-like treatment, her growls got her a seat.

As a result of her late arrival the taxi firm then initially added to the unpleasantness by saying that it was getting very late and they weren't sure if they could meet her – this was after having *specifically* agreed by phone to be available if necessary for a 24 hour operation. We'd taken as much care in advance as was possible to ensure her safety in all circumstances – but we'd still been confounded

About 01:00, part way through the summary above, I went out and obtained three more taxi numbers from a late-night bar (they're nearly all late-night bars) and started on a recovery plan. I received no answer from one of them, and one had obviously just woken up and said he wasn't a twenty four hour service although his advert said he was. Swine. The third said something about Toulouse, and that he was on a call. I had difficulty understanding exactly what was going on – we both had poor mobile signals – but he seemed a decent fellow and I made a note of his number. Eventually, the original firm agreed to honour the original deal, and I knew Erika was in traceable and hopefully trustworthy hands.

I was waiting downstairs when the taxi arrived and it was a great relief to have her properly involved in the plot. I showed her to her room and, with only a brief acknowledgement of the provisions, we both retired to get what sleep remained possible.

During the next day we bought essential replacement bits and bobs for Erika. Her rucksack eventually arrived at the hotel at 18:00 that day. We put both rucksacks together to see if there would be a fight but they seemed fairly compatible. I'd planned to send home the broken sack – its spirit seemed to have gone completely – and to carry on with the new one that Erika had brought out, and which British Airways had tried to lose. I hoped that the new sack was not going to be as belligerent as the first one, and for an awful moment I imagined that the reputation of the first one had spread through the baggage grapevine, and that the airline had deliberately tried to lose the new one as a defensive measure. Just in case.

The minutes of a planning meeting contained the following actions. We would do a very short stroll tomorrow afternoon to Juzet. The following day we would do the big one over the top from Juzet to Fos. That's eighteen and a half miles and over 5000 feet of ascent and descent. Non-trivial.

To make that first proper trek more enjoyable for Erika I decided that we would taxi the sacks to Fos tomorrow, so we could then walk light the following day.

My tired old rucksack would also approve of this I thought.

I booked beds at a small gîte or pension at Juzet for tomorrow night. It was named Le Poujastou and the lady in charge, Madame Cottereau, sounded very hospitable. I then booked a taxi for tomorrow on the recommendation of the tourist office – they did the phoning which was very helpful. This taxi driver turned out to be the one to whom I spoke when he was on a job to Toulouse during the early hours of the day of Erika's arrival. We eventually determined that he was in fact on his way back at the time and that he could have easily picked Erika up on the way. C'est la vie.

His name was something that sounded very much like *Jairdeece* and this was so close to the French pronunciation of GR10, that for Erika and myself he became Monsieur GR10.

He gave me a quote to deliver the rucksacks to the Hôtel la Gentilhommière at Fos. Unfortunately the gîte was full. This quote subsequently turned out to be spot on from his meter – we went for the ride there and back – and I considered that because no nett or overall progress was made by the taxi ride, it therefore didn't invalidate the principle of *walk all the way*.

It was grey all day with no sun. Cassoulet at lunchtime. Pétèran Luchonaise – trîpes d'Agneau, a local speciality in the evening. It wasn't as tasty as I'd expected. The sky was lightening, though tomorrow was not forecast to improve. The mountain guides that we'd visited in Bagnères-de-Luchon also gave a warning that the route to Fos can be dangerous. We will have to keep the bivvy bags with us, and take a good supply of food – just in case.

Day 35: Bagnères-de-Luchon to Juzet

The weather presented nothing better nor worse than mixed cloud with a little rain and a little sun, so, knowing that we had no more than about five easy miles to Juzet, we lurked around Bagnères-de-Luchon. It was a slightly rainy morning, and there seemed nothing better to do than drink coffee and have a simple lunch of moules et frites with a pichet of rouge out of the rain.

We taxied the sacks to Fos as planned, and when the weather picked up after lunch we took the Télécabine (cable car) up to Super-Bagnères and then walked down. The weather had made it too late to walk up and down. Coming down we encountered an eager-looking, bushy-bearded walker who told us that he hated the GR10 because of all the ups and downs. I nodded vigorously.

Later in the early evening we walked to Juzet, and on the way we passed a group playing a game with cast iron quoits. That was about as interesting as it got.

At Le Poujastou the hospitality and food was fantastic – root vegetable soup, a green bean and tomato course, and the crowning glory – my favourite meal anywhere in the world – Shepherd's Pie – and a good one. Fromage, cherry tart, coffee.

The husband of Madame Cottereau was a National Park Warden, and as we talked we realised that he had been one of the group playing the strange game that we'd earlier stopped to watch on the way here. It was a very pleasant mealtime with them and two other residents. Everyone talked enthusiastically about wildlife, mountains, the changing world, and Gypaètes. Madame Cottereau sees them in the region now and again.

There was a spotless large four bed dormitory to ourselves, and an excellent modern bathroom. After such a relaxing evening we slept excellently and there were no complaints the next day about snoring.

Day 36: Juzet to Fos
07:00 – 18:10

The breakfast at Le Poujastou was in character and included a cold porridge made with oats and banana. We were enthusiastically told that it was taken from a German recipe and that it was prepared overnight with no cooking. It was delicious and nutritious.

It was again *generally sunny* and not too hot. It would have been very tiring with normal rucksacks, and the descent to Fos was every bit as bad as Castle said it would be. Very slippery, and very long. We both fell many times – there seemed no way to avoid it, however careful we were.

From the wrist machine our normal rate of descent over some pasture land was working out at about nine metres per minute. I like to know these things. At one point, however, Erika saw some cows. She hates cows. She was off at a rate of descent of fourteen metres per minute.

There were stony tracks, grassy hillsides, hidden lakes and spectacular ridges. There were choices of route to suit the weather, and we had some good high-level views – both back to Bagnères-de-Luchon and ahead to the descent to Fos.

It was a pretty good, if hard, introduction to the GR10.

At one place it was very difficult to find the exit from a clearing, but, after a lot of walking in circles and searching around an area of bracken, we found the route. It had been concealed by bushes and dropped down and away through dense trees right at the entrance to the clearing.

That clearing had seemed to beckon and lure us away from the route. I'd almost been tempted to go by compass down through the trees at another point, and it later became apparent that if we'd done that it would have needed a lot of cross-country work through dense woods and up steep rocky hillsides to regain the route.

Never, never knowingly leave the route, I warned her.

Salade Perigourdine, confit de canard (Erika), entrecôte (me) – two portions of sautéed potatoes that we couldn't finish because I'd asked for a portion and one was included anyway.

Bagnères-de-Luchon, Haute-Garonne, Ariège

We were both pretty knackered from that long hard day, but at the end of the meal I paid up and we retired to a comfortable room with the intention of an 07:00 start in the morning.

Day 37: Fos to Étang d'Araing
10:00 – 18:45

Fos was still in the Haute-Garonne département, but today we would cross into the historic province of Couserans in the Ariège département

Being so tired from the previous day, (I'd gone soft in Bagnères-de-Luchon, and Erika had only just started, although she's very fit anyway) we totally failed to get out at the planned time. When we did get out, what a surprise, it was very hot and sunny. There was some shade though, and it wasn't too bad. I carried three litres of water which turned out to be totally unnecessary because there were good sources along the way.

It was a long hard day, the Pas du Bouc and Col d'Auéron never seemed to appear. It was a great relief when they did, and we had at that point some spectacular views over distant and receding mountain ranges.

Finally, we hit a summit and were in sight of the French tricolor flying over the CAF (Club Alpine Français) Refuge which was a few hundred feet below us. There was a big snowfield in the way but the *ballises* pointed round it to the north west, so a little way past that obstacle we stopped about twenty minutes short of the Refuge for an orange. An orange was always a high point of the day for me, but I liked to eat it in triumph with the objective either in sight or almost so.

Dominic, the guardian at the Refuge was fairly welcoming but asserted his patronship at any and every opportunity. He virtually turned away some walkers with a dog – he did actually turn them away, but they had had enough of him and were going anyway. They went and slept in a tent just behind some rocks. He then told us that they'd phoned earlier and had said they would arrive at a certain time – and then they were late. *Tsk tsk* he clicked – he would not tolerate such sloppiness.

Pasta, and excellent soupe à haricots et lardons. Saucisse and bread starter. Mars for pudding for Erika. We had been grudgingly allowed to cook within the refuge area, but were frowned at because we weren't having the meal that was being cooked for one or two other walkers. We were not allowed to leave even a small bag of rubbish – though he accepted an empty coke can for scrap. He then laboriously explained that *...in the mountains we have to take our rubbish with us...*

We knew this well enough, all refuse has to be helicoptered or donkeyed away to the civilisation services many miles distant. We were respectful of the mountains by instinct and we didn't need the lecture – a simple *No* would have done. They burned paper waste at the CAF Refuges anyway, and that was mainly what we wanted to leave.

A final peculiarity at this refuge was the temperature control for the showers. This seemed to be determined by Dominic. You went in the shower – assuming you were lucky enough to catch it in a tolerable temperature range to start with – then, according to your shouts, squeals, or grunts, Dominic made the adjustments. Other than the yells, the *showeree* played no part in determining the temperature. This worked after a fashion when there was only one person, and when Dominic had time to listen. If there was a crowd, or the satellite phone rang, there was a great danger of being either frozen to death, or boiled alive, since the master control freak couldn't possibly have known which squeal meant hotter, which meant colder, or even which squeal went with which water control valve wheel. No doubt there was a reason in the controller's mind to account for this level of interference, but when you are on the receiving end of such domineering nonsense – well, it's disconcerting to say the least.

Despite the negativity of its warden, the views from this refuge were stunning. It was very remote, and very beautiful – a must see for anyone fortunate enough to be in the area.

Day 38: Étang d'Araing to Sentein and Bornac
10:00 – 16:00

Very hot and sunny with good shade throughout the day.

It should have been an easy quick descent after our citron tea, and honey with pain complét – that type of bread travels so much better than normal baguettes. Dominic again grudgingly sold me two jus d'oranges.

"They're supposed to be with the full CAF petit déjeuner," he miserably intoned.

Shortly afterwards he cosied up with the couple he'd turned away yesterday, and ingratiated himself with them when they bought his coffee. We thanked him profusely for his hospitality – I narrowly avoided adding Mon Capitaine – and he puffed himself up, and made a small speech about how he enjoyed his custody of that area of the Pyrénées. You could almost hear la Marseillaise in the background, and I wondered if I should kiss him on each cheek, and offer a medal.

Stiff, formal, and unfriendly are the words which summarise that martinet. He should have been a traffic warden, not a CAF Refuge warden.

To get to Sentein where transport could be joined we needed at this part of the GR10 to follow a different *ballise* leading north of northeast. It was yellow and red which always indicates a local trail rather than a long distance one. It was part of the Tour du Biros.

We lost the trail at one place because it was much more poorly marked than the GR10 highway, and this added about four or five kilometres to our day's journey. The spot at which we went wrong actually had a directional sign which, with hindsight, I later understood. I should have looked more closely at the map when we were there, and I would then have known the correct trail. The incorrect path took us to see la refuge de la Chapelle de l'Isard – a pleasant little diversion I thought. It's often the case that in spite of losing the intended trail, clear-headed use of the compass, and an almost instinctive choice will get you through. This was the case later on down the wrong trail in the region of la Chapelle de l'Isard.

By this time I could tell by studying the map and by looking at the compass and the surroundings what the overall picture was; and whether the route, even if not the ideal one, was going to turn out OK or not. It seemed to me that mistakes were usually made by a momentary lack of attention, rather than as a wrong decision when all the information was presented. A few days later this was again proved to me when, in spite of my own instincts, I followed someone else and we all got almost hopelessly lost. I think this is known as the exception proving the rule. In that later case I actually had a 90% certain idea of where we were – but I assumed the others knew better. Never follow someone else.

Anyway, back in the present we dropped down past many empty, spooky hamlets until we came out on the road to Sentein. There were many dilapidated wooden houses and outbuildings alongside the small river that slowly descended and traced the route taken by the GR10 in its local alias of the Tour du Biros.

As we walked – almost tip-toed – past the deserted settlements it was easy to imagine some savage recluse or hermit watching us from the depths of a shadowy and now stale and damp living room – a once gaily lit home where Christmas would have been celebrated for decades by a thriving family. I could just picture its last resident now – grey-haired and wasted, an unwashed and unshaven creature with sunken eyes, lurking behind a dirty window and twitching the grimy moth-eaten curtains; a vagabond in a relic left over from an earlier era, now left with nothing but sadness, bitterness, and regret – and maybe a rat for dinner. It was a post-apocalyptic vision within a wider and more persistent idyll.

It was with more than a little relief that we re-entered civilisation in the region of Sentein, although that village had nothing at all to commend it – there was no open shop, no café, or any sort of hostelry. The person on duty at the Mairie in Sentein, a man with whom we spoke at some length, was very helpful in establishing that the gîte at Bornac which was further down the road was open. He also helped us find out that the bus would stop there, although the *horaires* (timetable) indicated that it stopped at Sentein only.

Le Relais Montagnard at Bornac – an excellent gîte.

We found the bus stop and established that it was a *By Request Only* stop at Bornac – that's why it wasn't listed in the schedule at the Mairie. Must remember that in future. The available buses also allowed Erika to get the 13:20 instead of the 06:55 car privé (small local bus service) to Saint-Girons where there was an SNCF bus terminus. The SNCF bus then goes to Boussens where an SNCF train then connects to Toulouse for the flight out. This option was the only possibility given the geographic and time constraints. Pyrénéan public transport can be tricky – if you are lucky enough to find it at all.

This initial exposure to the Ariège was salutary – there were many deserted / empty / decrepit buildings, and an impression of wholesale *desertification*. This French term aptly describes the notion of people leaving and the conversion of once proud and happy homes into deserts.

The town of Sentein, with nothing whatsoever to offer except a helpful Mairie, just added to this impression of loss. What would the real deep Ariège be like? I decided I didn't want to find out on this trip, and that I would dip into it from a better supported road route like Philippe had intended. There was no shame in this, I reassured myself, the main objective was always to walk ocean to ocean through the mountains. That's what I'm doing. The GR10 itself is, overall, a recent and arbitrary integration of smaller undoubtedly autonomous and ancient links between adjacent communities. It's now a contemporary leisure trail, the route of which seems to change annually, and the idea of taking that route for trade between the two coasts seems to me very unlikely. I wasn't trading but I wasn't part of one of the local communities either. I'd go whichever way I wanted to go – so there! – and with a Leki pole I knocked the seed head off a dandelion for good measure, sending dozens of small fluffy weedlings into the still air.

Now at this instant I realised that no-one else was taking part in this silent argument that I was having with myself, and that I'd lost the thread. I looked at Erika to see if she'd noticed, but I don't think she did.

Later that night I saw what looked like a small blackhead on my leg. I tried squeezing it with no luck and I didn't think much more about it. It was on the inside of my thigh.

At about 18:00, while sitting with a beer, I noticed with horror a small beetle or tick emerging from my leg. It was not an attractive sight – the tick thing that is. I pulled it out and tried squashing it between my fingertips but it was a hard little blighter. I succeeded in crushing it on the table with a fingernail, and it gave a satisfying pop and a splat. I told Erika.

"*Uuurgh*, what's that," she said, pointing to another less tenacious one that I again managed to pull out intact – I hope. I'm now watching several red patches for any evidence of leftovers. I Dabbed all areas with iodine. I don't know if they were sheep ticks, deer ticks, or something picked up from one of the secretive writhing blankets I thought had avoided me in refuges.

Rice and tuna, fish in foil, Îsles flôttante, tarte aux pommes, and all washed down with a fine and special (locally produced) prune eau de Ville that I had in a very conspiratorial session with le patron and a splendid group of locals in the bar.

Selected Photograph Bagnères-de-Luchon

Day 33 – 15 June 12:00

Bagnères-de-Luchon.

8   Couserans, Ariège
Day 39: Rest at Bornac

Hot and sunny, and tout seule encore (alone again).

Strange empty day. The kind patron gave Erika a lift to Saint-Girons, and when he got back, he had a note and a cigar from ma petite. Erika had given him some money and asked him to choose a good cigar for me since I had just innocently let it drop in conversation that a cigar would be great one of these evenings. I hadn't thought any more of it, but she'd obviously remembered. I pulled out my handkerchief and blew my nose loudly. I think one of those damn flies just flew in my eye.

I walked around Bornac – there was not a lot to see, and so I lay in the sun by the lake most of the day. I've no idea why I didn't carry on walking somewhere that day, I just didn't feel like it. It was a fortuitous decision.

A large group of Americans arrived and were great company. I felt quite honoured when they invited me to speak to their group for a while about my experiences so far. They were going into Spain to attend a religious festival in Catalonia. One girl had thick tape on her heel which, by adding a great thick extra skin, helped to stop blisters even getting a start. I'd never thought of this, and although I'd only developed blisters while wearing the over-sized Millet boots, it seemed worth noting in the log.

At the end of the experience it was interesting to realise that my choice of a good quality lining sock with a good quality thick woollen sock, together with correctly sized boots, had seen me through with no other blisters at all.

During the evening a large crowd of diners was making merry, and a local scavenging dog was begging and getting fed from the table by one of the Americans, when another group of French diners arrived with a dog. Without warning there was a spectacular dog fight, and this was almost followed by a punch-up among the guests when it was at first believed that the local beggar dog was with some of them. The proprietor of the gîte came to the rescue, explained the situation, and then rewarded the scavenger with a bowl of scraps, just out of sight of the new arrival. I looked on knowingly. Dogs seemed to be at the centre of many of the incidents I recalled along the way.

Australian Ed (from Pembrokeshire, Wales) and his friend Michel (from Pau, France) arrived. It was quite odd because we were all chatting in French and it was only after five or ten minutes that Ed and I realised we weren't French.

They'd started from Hendaye on the 29th May and, in spite of them being in their sixties, they were virtually running the route and sometimes combining two stages in a single day. They were talking about the same ploy as me to avoid the Ariège cabins if possible – almost the same route. They borrowed my map and were talking about the GR10 leaving Bornac. This was a surprise to me because I was expecting to be walking along roads for a while from here. It turned out that one of the famous GR10 variants was marked in Michel's Topoguide, but not as such on my map or in Castle.

After our earlier experience with the Tour du Biros I was a bit reluctant to follow another local trail that might not be well way-marked, although later on the journey, I did this more than once without any problem and, compared to some of my earlier snow-covered stretches that had been effectively unmarked for several kilometres, I thought I was being ridiculously over-cautious at Bornac.

Puff-pastry cases containing a mixture of goat cheese and honey – superb. Chicken casserole and pasta, fromage, bed. I hardly slept at all that night, Ed and Michel said the same next morning. Perhaps the rich food was a bit too much.

Day 40: Bornac to Esbints
06:50 – 15:00

After Ed and Michel had told me about their rate of progress and of their intention to get the walk completed as soon as possible I had some reservations about setting out with them. I remembered keeping up with Klaus. Still, I thought, I'm probably fitter now, so we'll have a go. We crept out of the gîte in the early morning silence after a good petit déjeuner.

Hot, sunny, some shade. We were plagued by horse flies by the squadron, they were a real menace. We walked without stopping for a long, long way, and when I remarked on it, breathlessly, Ed and Michel said that was their style and that they didn't stop very often. It was quite tiring and I thought I didn't like the style, but I did it and made much better than published times. They were a formidable pair and, with my lazy style, I felt a bit out of place. On one long ascent the subject of French film making cropped up, and Ed gave me a very long description, in French, of the plots of *Jean de Florette*, and of *Manon des Sources*, neither of which I'd seen at that time. His discourse was in French so that Michel could affirm the detail. The impressive aspect of all this was the way he kept talking as we climbed more and more steeply, not exactly without a bit of puffing, but he kept it up for many minutes. I was getting exhausted just concentrating on the French.

Michel had no map and no compass – just a guide book. He hurtled off through the woods outside the gîte, and a couple of times we had to retrace our steps – it was only impenetrable undergrowth that finally seemed to arrest him. He'd just collide with a herbaceous wall like a wrestler hitting the ropes, then turn about and career off in another direction.

Michel, who later on was behind Ed and myself, missed the sign to the gîte at Esbints that was on the track, and apparently ended up at another gîte in Aunac several kilometres further on. Efforts to get him back failed.

Pasta and soup. There was a plaster cast of an awesome bear paw print on the wall. The gîte owner was a berger, and his daughter told us that he had heard a bear near his sheep about five days ago. This was only a couple of kilometres from where we were, and there was a fantastic remote feeling here. The berger's daughter and son were running the place while the mother was ill in hospital. I got the impression from their conversation that this was not a physical ailment, but some sort of depression from the remoteness of the region.

I found two more of the tick things on the same leg, dug at another suspect with needle and knife, and then iodined the lot. I got iodine on my clothes and hands and was in a real multicoloured mess. Thinking that I was permanently stained, it was quite a pleasant surprise to find that it all washed away easily. My leg bled badly after this surgery and it was unbearably hot in the dormitory.

Day 41: Esbints to Rouze
06:30 – 11:00

Up at 05:30. We made a beeline for Rouze. There was some cloud, sunny later. Clouding over again at 15:30. We met the errant Michel in Aunac at 07:00 as Ed had arranged with him by phone between the two gîtes. We had fantastic views of the distant Mont Valier and the surrounding wall of mountains. On one very steep part of the trail I got the impression that Michel and I were in a race. We hurtled up a steep nightmarish stony path, sweat pouring down, and breath coming in shorter and shorter gasps, and I just about beat him – only just. I told him I'd never done anything like that in my life before, I'd barely managed to gasp it out, and he clapped me on the back.

"Bravo!" he said, laughing. He really was a dynamo.

The gîte at Rouze was really isolated and, while no meals were provided, we bought wine, goat cheese, pate, and some delicious terrine which had been made at the gîte.

Wine, bread, soft cheese, pate...., oh and I almost forgot the wine. What more did we need?

Flies were even more horrendous and numerous. Horse flies had again been insufferable on the way here, and now house flies came outdoors to join us as well while we sat and lay basking in the sun. It was the worst place for flies yet, although strangely and thankfully they didn't seem to return inside the gîte with us. Maybe they were really garden flies.

The lady owner and her baby were looking after the gîte while her husband worked elsewhere during the day. She'd studied at university, and the two of them had bought the gîte as a business after the previous owner packed up. Like the Swiss some days earlier, she also recommended the GR20 in Corsica as one of the most beautiful of the GR series. I mentioned that the Swiss had said that water was very difficult to find there, and that the first task of each day was to divine it, and fill up the containers. She totally contradicted this view and said water was in plentiful supply. So, I thought at the time, the only way to resolve this is to go and find out. After I survive the current madness that is.

For dinner, we contrived a feast from the victuals we'd purchased at the gîte, and we shared out my soup and pasta as well. We had a banquet, and a great deal of light-hearted badinage went on as the wine took it's inevitable stranglehold on reason and good manners.

It was at some time during this pleasant mealtime and soaring familiarity that I had cause, I can't remember why, to say something odd to Michel, in French.

"What are you, man or mouse?"

He certainly wasn't offended by this, and he laughed and shrugged his shoulders. Ed and myself then took great pleasure explaining the meaning of the expression, and the correct response from any self-confident and self-respecting recipient of this jibe – possibly accompanied by a smoothing of the whiskers.

"After you with the cheese my good fellow!" I told him, "that is the correct response," and then he saw the joke.

Under the caresses of the wine, and as we passed the real cheese, this seemed like a masterpiece of *Entente Cordiale*.

This was however, to be *La nuit de la bète* – The Night of the Beast as I termed it. Our dormitory was remote from the main house, and there were just us three in residence. Remember this was miles from anywhere.

About 03:00 I was woken by a wild animal screeching horribly just outside the external door that went from my room to the *garden* i.e. the mountain. This was followed almost immediately by what I thought was a loud and furious series of movements within the gîte, and I honestly thought the others were fighting something. I imagined some miscreant taking on the other two, while the frustrated ranting of it's partner, the creature outside my door, told me it had been a good idea to lock it before retiring for the night. I'd been tempted to leave it unlocked when I felt I was being a wimp, but now I was glad I hadn't.

As I advanced towards the other internal door to the landing, poles and knife at the ready – like an idiot I'd forgotten the chilli – I realised the noise had died down, and imagined two gory dismembered corpses with a victorious, hideously humped, and grey-stubbled cross between a wild boar and Gordon Brown standing over them. Gordon Brown was the Chancellor of the Exchequer at the time of the incident. The red-eyed beast would have slowly turned its head to look at me with a grin, displaying slivers of human tissue in its teeth like you get from a good lamb chop.

I carefully opened my door and I saw that their door was open and that they were both awake. They thought the sight of me, armed to the teeth, was hilarious, and they said they had heard nothing. Now, I know that there had been something scrabbling at the outside door, and something had been resisting capture at the foot of the stairs – and why were they so wide awake at 03:00?

I peered down into the dark depths of the stairwell but there was nothing to be seen. The previous night I'd gone to sleep alone in the kitchen area in case of any snoring competition. I returned there now, with the distinct impression that something very fishy was going on. I only half-slept for the remainder of that night.

Day 42: Rouze to Aulus-les-Bains
08:00 – 18:15

This was a horror journey to follow a night of horror. It was too hot, too fast, and too long. I was following the others and we all went wrong. Michel was in front and storming along without map or compass – as he usually does.

Before that though, we had, fairly early on, climbed steeply for about 450 metres without a stop in one hour. I felt great. Then, at Michel's suggestion we stopped at about 11:30 for a midday meal at Saint-Lizier. After the initial good progress, this seemed, over an initial beer, like an excellent idea, though it was something I'd never done before. We ate outside, in the blazing sun but under a sunshade, and did we eat. Charcuterie to start, followed by an enormous côte d'agneau, chips, cheese, ice-cream, wine…. As we ate we listened to the evocative tones of Charles Trênét singing La Mer, drifting across a neighbouring garden. Hovering at a respectable distance from our table, the comforting, glorious sentinel presence of the Pyrénéan ranges seemed quite benign. What an atmosphere!

Now, eating like this is not my normal style. Well, to be precise, it's exactly my style, but not my time. When walking, I prefer to eat very lightly, if at all, during the day, and to take an evening meal, although not too late. It was now too hot. It was much too hot. I had eaten and drunk far too much, and what I really needed, was a really long nap. So what do we do? About 13:00 as we approached the hottest hours of the day we set off. Not for the last time, I wanted to flatten my ears and whine and grizzle again, but I couldn't show the weakness.

When we went wrong I knew it. We'd just left the road onto a track. I had the compass and map and I took some bearings.

"Look here fellers, this can't be right, we shouldn't be able to see that village over there on a bearing like this," I said.

I held out the compass for them to see. There was a brief discussion that took about three seconds, and Michel shot off again with a dismissive wave of the hand, followed by Ed.

Like a weak-willed lamb I followed.

That was a big mistake. We had left the road and had been following a yellow / red *ballise*, not the GR10. This was deliberate, and I knew we were expecting a turn to the north towards the Col – it should have been about one kilometre to the Col. After a while the *ballises* dried up, but no-one commented on it – we were all being idiotic. A moment's study of the map would have shown the error clearly. This was the sort of circumstance I'd foreseen long before commencing the walk, and the main reason why I'd determined to do it on my own. You can never blame anyone else when things go badly for a democratically (usually more like anarchically) convened group. When you're on your own you take more care.

I could now understand how a lemming might feel just as he was going over the cliff-edge and, looking round at all the other eager but dumb faces; he might well exclaim, "hang on a minute lads..."

After much scrambling and falling through thick undergrowth and trees when the slim path we were on disappeared completely, we finally emerged, dry as a bone on a steep grassy hillside in full sun. With some difficulty and slithering, we traversed this for some way on the same contour, then descended again to the left towards some trees for shade. We now had no idea where we were, why we were there, or where we were going. As my contribution I now refused to look at the map and, to no-one in particular, I muttered.

"Let's see you get out of this one."

We now squelched through an unwholesome, shady, marshy area, that developed into flat grey-ish silt that stank, and suggested the outflow of a septic tank, and sure enough, after a little way we emerged at a house that was being renovated, seemingly with no road access. In spite of the lack of highway, there was an off-road vehicle parked nearby – I supposed that it was an off-road vehicle because it was off the road, and there was no road. This seemed like a brilliant deduction at the time, and I wanted to shout eureka. I think I was getting delirious from a combination of excessive marsh gas, and water deprivation, and I distinctly remember feeling that I wanted to be somewhere else.

At the house we were warmly welcomed by an enormous dog that snarled and had such well-matched enormous teeth that it could have won a talent contest if it hadn't been so hairy. Only the fact that we outnumbered it, and that it was so stupid that it couldn't decide who was the weakest, prevented the onset of a war of one-sided attrition that would have seen us individually picked off from the rear quarters as we scuttled back to the septic tank. I didn't like the way it looked us over and seemed to rest it's gaze momentarily longer on me. I gave a slight shake of the head, and pointed a pole at Michel, mouthing the words *eat him*, while turning my head, all the time making sure that I didn't lose the eye-contact that once regrettably formed cannot be broken. I was looking for a tree with low enough branches to allow a quick ascent. I couldn't find one, and I thought that anyway, if I had, it would only have been useful as long as they didn't also have a house-bear. Or at least as long as it wasn't a black bear that can climb trees. A grizzly bear would be fine since they can't climb. Or was it the other way round? I'd read it earlier in the trip in Bill Bryson's book, but couldn't now remember which was which.

Thankfully, instead of a bear, the smiling house owner appeared in the nick of time, and he allowed me to give a demonstration of a hydro-electric turbine at a water standpipe that the enormous teeth with the hairy dog attached had seemed so reluctant to surrender.

Somewhat recovered, and now willing to share the map again, I showed it to the house owner and asked him if *this*, jabbing the map with a trembling digit, was where we were. He confirmed this to the silent glowering applause from the others, and also told us that there was no really easy way out of there. There were two possibilities, both difficult. He didn't even seem to comprehend how we'd arrived. The best way was back to the road we'd left some hours earlier, but via a tree-shaded, and not too badly surfaced path. By not too badly surfaced, it turned out that he meant we wouldn't need climbing gear.

We were back about two hours and two miles later, on the road at exactly the place where we had left it. This was just after having seen the clear north turn marked by a yellow and red *ballise* that we had stormed past, maybe three or four hours previously. As we reached it, we stopped at that north-pointing track and looked at each other. No words were necessary to express the desire to stay with the certainty of the road. Michel grunted and lurched towards the road.

It was another nightmare on the uphill road in the heat to the Col de Latrape just before Aulus. I took a very long time moving from one solitary tree-shaded spot, a hundred metres maybe to the next one, resting there for several minutes, and then repeating the process. After the Col there was still a four kilometre descent into Aulus.

The other two are now talking about getting up at 05:00 to avoid the heat. Why am I doing this? To make things worse, I found that on the rare occasions that I had a phone signal, my phone didn't work any more. I couldn't call out. BT had been completely unhelpful – rude and arrogant even, and the problem, Lesley had told me, could only be resolved by me calling BT. There was just a piece of sweaty cheese for tea at the gîte d'étape and again the black clouds seemed to be gathering.

The Ariège is awful, I'm only halfway across and the heat will get worse. Today was very, very bad and it still looks bad for the next few days. I've no phone, the phone card is unreliable, and I found another tick today. Ed had one as well. The flies were even worse if that's possible – horse flies were increasing in number.

It all looked pretty bad again when I got to Aulus.

Day 43: Rest at Aulus-les-Bains

I didn't get up early and I'd slept very badly. Such poor sleep often seems to follow a day of intense heat and exertion. It certainly was not hot during the night. Ed and Michel went at about 05:30. I bought some fruit, soup, and eggs for a light lunch and evening meal.

At the Thermes I was informed courteously that it was only possible to try drinking different spring waters, and that it was not possible to actually get in the water – public use of the baths was restricted to the weekend.

The Thermes here seemed very sterile and could be anywhere – there was no feeling of spirit of place or naturalness whatsoever – I hoped Ax-les-Thermes would be better; it might be my last chance for a bathe.

To the dismay of some of my sun-wary friends I normally soak up any amount of severe sunshine, but it was so very hot again that I found I couldn't stay outside after about 15:45 without roasting. I will need to start early tomorrow like the others did today.

You can't blame anyone when a disaster like yesterday occurs, but I shall be happier on my own, at my own pace, and responsible only to myself. Walking round the town when it was cooler I visited a church and paid my respects at a war memorial. Like all such memorials, particularly in France, this one was crammed with the names of some of those who didn't complete their walk through World Wars One and Two. Being always very moved at these speechlessly strident reminders I spent some very reflective moments.

It was in Aulus, a while after contemplating the memorial, that I saw the second three-legged dog in a week. The first one had a front leg missing, the second had the back left missing, and I thought this was definitely an omen of some sort. I glanced up to see if there were any black birds passing from either side. I knew it was OK if they came from one side but not the other, only again, like yesterday's house-bear problem, I couldn't remember which was OK. Fortunately there weren't any on either side.

I sat on the parapet of a bridge trying to work out what all this might mean, got absolutely nowhere with it, and decided to try some anti-insect spray hoping it might repel the ticks and other nasties, and anything that two three-legged dogs could portend.

To pass the time I spent some time doing a survey of insect sprays – prices and claims – and a lady in one of the shops gave me an anti-insect recipe consisting of garlic, lemon, and vinegar. While this was natural and traditional, and I love the ingredients, I didn't want to be lumbered with a bottle of vinegar, a string of garlic, and a bag of lemons, so I regrettably chose a spray container of something that later turned out to be more deadly to me than any insect.

I sat and made my reserve plan for the morrow – if there was a late ascent, particularly in hot weather I'd take a break at the Port de Saleix and then stay at the Refuge de Bassiès.

While getting some provisions I found Philippe was also in Aulus, and we were just talking when I received a call from Lesley telling me yet more of the extreme arrogance and rudeness of BT. Before I left home I believed that I had established a direct debit facility with them so that my mobile bill would automatically be managed in my absence. They failed to do this, didn't advise me of their failure, and then simply cut my connection without warning. They then refused to allow Lesley to rectify the problem, and I was obliged to phone them from Aulus and pay the bill to get the connection reset. They wouldn't listen to Lesley or even speak to her about her own account either. After about an hour we established that a password would have enabled her to sort it, but they didn't tell her that. We both knew the password but it was never even requested. I was furious and wanted to cancel all of my BT accounts on return.

Meeting Philippe had confirmed my plan to go to the Refuge de Bassiès, he was going there and is great company. Bernard another Frenchman who also arrived at the gîte today, was joining the party.

Waking very early and in a medical mood I dug at my leg again at about 05:30 and made another hole in it without getting anything. I felt the dreadful tick was burrowing deeper as I dug at it with the knife.

This lunacy would probably have needed a local anaesthetic at home, but the imagined horrors of the things eating through my leg – this during the morning anxiety time – spurred me on.

Day 44: Aulus-les-Bains to Refuge de Bassiès
07:15 – 12:45

It was extremely hot again after 10:30.

I'd developed a terribly bad neck after I'd sprayed anti-moustiques (fly repellent) on my sunburned skin. I reckoned that such repellent should only be used while wearing a full chemical / biological warfare protection or Hazchem suit it was so nasty. Of course, such a suit would render the spray redundant, unless the insects were inside the suit. But then I'd need two suits, I thought, one inside the other, and it wasn't very likely that there would be even one such suit in a place like Aulus. I was on the point of going open loop as they say in control theory mathematics, with visions of nested Russian dolls dressed in such suits, and the images you get between two mirrors, where there is an infinitely receding world that you can't quite see because your own head gets in the way.

From this self-induced hallucination I was saved by, of all things, a horse fly. It bit me while I was distracted, the swine. It bit me so hard, that I shouted first in English, and then, with an expletive in French so it would understand its last sounds. I slapped it as hard as I could. Of course the sun-burned and chemically treated piece of leg that had apparently attracted instead of repelling the horsefly, and that had suffered the bite, now got slapped as well, and further reddened. I just managed to suppress a series of words that should never be spoken together. In fact they shouldn't be spoken individually either in polite company. Instead I made a sort of hissing creaking noise, a bit like an over-inflated leather bladder about to explode, and counted from one to five hundred and twelve in binary.

Aulus had once been a centre for Montreurs d'Ours – the men who captured and then showed bears at markets, and who made them perform for the entertainment of the crowds. There were several old photographs around the town of that undesirable cruelty. The usual pose is a muzzled bear on a rope, standing beside a vertical rough staff, with one paw placed on the top, and one on the side. From a population of some hundreds at the beginning of the twentieth century, a survey made a couple of decades ago, had suggested that there were about seven left. That's not a printing error, it's 7, i.e. less than ten!

It was with some surprise that I later read in a book at the gîte at Mérens that a survey now suggested about forty. Had the first survey been wrong? had the bears themselves reversed their demographically challenged state? or had some other agency been involved? As I already knew, the French government is re-introducing brown bears to the region, mainly it seems, from The Czech Republic or Slovakia.

Walking with Bernard and Philippe was good. They were usually in front, and we made 500 metres ascent in an hour and a half with no stopping, and did a Castle section specified as three and a half hours in two and three quarter hours. Things were looking good.

As we passed on our way after stopping to speak with a couple who had been coming towards us, there was an obligatory exchange of the GR10 farewell protocol – *bon courage* from one party, and *bon continuation* from the other. I think Philippe rolled his eyes at these exchanges, feeling they were a bit of a cliché. Being an outsider though, I loved it, and took every chance to either originate the exchange, or to respond to it. What a plonker.

I sat at Port de Saleix for about half an hour, simply to enjoy the scenery, while Philippe and Bernard continued on at their break-neck pace. This was a bad mistake. I should have just paused for five minutes. The heat built up and I was frazzled by the time I arrived at the CAF refuge. The back of my neck was an enormous mass of blisters where the anti-insect spray had reacted with the sunburn, and this had been made worse by my collar that had rubbed it raw. It was so painful I couldn't turn my head, and I didn't sleep again that night. I didn't see any more ticks, but the hole in my leg was a reminder. If you didn't get them quickly they just went deeper I admonished myself.

Philippe and Bernard were a couple of crag hoppers and they set a cracking pace. Bernard had leg veins that were bigger than the rest of his leg, and he carried a plastic bottle of water in one hand all the time. As he walked he held it out like a counterweight. I was pleased at one point when, for all their stamina, they shot past a right-turn *ballise* and I managed to call them back from a false path.

With Philippe I'd planned a cabin tour through the rest of the Ariège in spite of earlier misgivings – I was concerned that this seemed to indicate a growing tendency towards masochism.

The prefabricated steel Bassiès refuge was magnificently situated in high, rugged and rocky surroundings far from any road or track. There were views to the west up higher valleys from which rivers now issued at maximum rates from the melting snow that still covered most of the mountain sides and peaks. There were cirques, or walls of rock, and down-valley views to the south-east where stunted pines heralded the distant tree-line. There were great waterfalls swollen by the high snow melt and, amidst all this, the guardian with his children and dogs frolicked in clear pools edged with tough springy turf where the river spread across the plateau and slowed into pebbly shallows.

It was unforgettable, and I resolved to return to it one day.

Of course every silver lining has a cloud with it, and in this case the cloud was a cloud of Tâons. I hadn't seen this latest curse before. Tâons are a pretty-looking greenish blue fly. One landed on my leg, and I was just thinking something like *oh beautiful colourful fly, what a pleasant life you have in this land of milk and honey*, when the swine bit me. They have a bite every bit as enjoyable as the black horse-flies, and we've been told that mosquitoes keep up the entertainment after dark.

Bernard is the original interrupting pest. He'd join any conversation while a speaker was in full flow, and just keep talking over the top while the first speaker attempted to keep to his line. He was monumentally insensitive. It had to be seen to be believed that he could interrupt, and then continue to talk as both he and the original speaker gradually raised their voices without actually appearing to take offence. When they both stopped, no-one really knew what had been said or who's turn was next. So they'd both start again simultaneously. This would happen a couple of times until Bernard won. He won every time.

The hosts were great but the food was a bit mediocre, although there was lots of it. After the food we played a game they called Tarot. This was a variant of whist, but played with a full Tarot pack of fifty six minor cards, plus twenty two major cards. That's seventy eight cards between four people – and you use all of them.

The familiar pack of fifty two cards is a subset of the Tarot's fifty six. The Tarot has a Page, Knight, Queen and King in each suit, while we commonly reduce this to Jack, Queen and King. The twenty two major cards feature individual characters or mysterious concepts, and they all have special significance – both alone and in combination with other cards. They include the well-known Hanged or Suspended Man, and the Death Card – neither of which necessarily signifies anything unpleasant. I tried to ignore the imagery that all these cards conjured up.

Now, I knew something of the Tarot as a clairvoyant's tool of the trade, but I didn't understand the bidding / contract rules of the game we were playing. They tried to explain the rules several times, but my French was inadequate. At last I managed to grasp enough to play defensively with two other players against one aspiring player, but it was a complete farce and they were very tolerant. It was a good job we weren't playing for money. The other players were Bernard, Philippe, and a guy called Davide.

Selected Photographs Couserans

Day 44 – 26 June 09:09
The view back to Aulus-les-Bains – somewhere down in the mist.

Day 44 – 26 June 17:07
A view from the Refuge de Bassiès.

Day 44 – 26 June 17:07
A view from the Refuge de Bassiès. Stunning all round.

Day 44 – 26 June 17:16
The setting of the Refuge de Bassiès.

9   Andorre, Haute Ariège
Day 45: Refuge de Bassiès to Capoulet-et-Junac
08:30 – 16:00

Thick mist, drizzle, soaked again. Bernard and Philippe are a couple of racing-goats as well as crag-hoppers. They set a crazy pace down from Bassiès. Even they were sliding and almost falling. I almost wasn't falling, and so I was getting pretty annoyed, and I decided to just slow down. We all got to Vicdessous about 11:30 and found Davide already there by a route he'd told us about, but which we'd decided to avoid because of mist and unfamiliarity. At a bar in Vicdessous, Philippe almost lost FFr300 when it fell from his pocket and fluttered under the table. The honest locals handed it in.

It was in this bar that I read in a local newspaper, a report on the death of two brown bears. They were said to have fallen over a cliff! I wondered why they didn't just say they'd fallen from an upstairs window after an all-night party, it would have been about as likely. Does anyone believe a bear would be so stupid as to *fall* over a cliff?

At the Vicdessous tourist office I found information on a chambre d'hôte at the small village of Capoulet some miles down the road. The tourist office phoned for me, and I spoke to a Madame Da Silva to ensure she was open and had a vacancy, otherwise I'd have stayed at Vicdessous.

From Vicdessous, Bernard went to Andorra by bus to buy new boots after his sole began to detach itself. His boots weren't made by Scarpa I noticed. Davide went off to get the car that he'd left in Vicdessous since his circular walk was now over, and Philippe and I set off to Laramade where we would part – he to three or four days of cabannes, me to cut to Mérens-les-Val, since I'd decided there was no leeway on the twelfth when my son Chris was arriving to walk the last few stages with me. There was constant drizzle and I got another soaking on the way to the chambre d'hôte. There was no dinner here, so I cooked pasta in my room because it was still monsooning outside. Sardines and cheese with pasta was a great way to end the day I reckoned; and sitting on the balcony after the rain, was a good way of watching the local farmers clearing up after the deluge.

I intended an early start the next day, and since Madame Da Silva didn't have change when I paid her, she agreed to leave FFr80 on the breakfast tray for me when she got it from her husband. I thought I might take the Thermos as compensation if she didn't. That was a wretched thought because she was very considerate, and of course left my change with the breakfast. I made yet another mental effort to try and harbour generous thoughts.

Day 46: Capoulet-et-Junac to Ax-les-Thermes
07:00 – 17:30

There was good shade to a place called Les Cabannes, and it was sunny after that, but not too hot. It was a very long day, about twenty-five miles with an amount of climbing and descending as well.

Starting at an altitude of 560 metres, the route rose rapidly to about 1160 metres, and then dropped back down to about 485 metres over a distance of about ten miles, and in only about four hours – i.e. by 11:00. Back in the Basque country this would have taken me all day and left me shattered. On this day, I carried on for another fifteen miles.

In one small hamlet where some renovation work was taking place, a cement mixer lorry was blocking the road where it passed between two houses. There was about two centimetres spare each side, and reflecting on the Napoleonic drive for standardisation, I asked the driver's mate if they had a national standard small road size and if that had been used as the basis for the national standard lorry width. He said it probably had.

Wild cherries were abundant in the area alongside tracks and roads, and a couple of signs had indicated prohibition concerning them, using the word *ramasser*. Now I know that word can mean collect, so on the basis that I wasn't intending to start a collection, I had a feast instead. It didn't say anything about not being able to do that.

Stopping for a coffee at Les Cabannes, I wondered while I sat with another friendly dog outside a bar, whether I should get a beard trim and a hair cut. I was beginning to look a bit like a troll, but the dog didn't attempt to molest me, so I decided not to, and set off to dodge traffic on the final approach to Ax.

To avoid part of the main N20 road I took a mixture of small roads and sentiers (paths), some parts of which were known as *La Tour de Val d'Ax*. There were many such delightful walks that could be taken at any time without the wholesale commitment to a coast to coast walk. However, the N20 couldn't be completely avoided if I was to get to Ax by 19:00 so, after a relaxing orange and Perrier at le Castelet, I entered the traffic zone. I was fairly tired by Ax but very glad to have done it in one day. That meant a nice short trip to Mérens the following day, and so I wouldn't need a very early start whatever the weather. The approach to Ax looked grim – all heavy industry and drab buildings – but the centre with its casino, church, and hotels is really excellent. At least, sitting with a beer where I'm writing this log book it is.

I could have eaten a small Pyrénéan mountain bear at this time and, from my balcony that overlooked the small town square, I noticed there was a good-looking eating spot next to the bar below the hotel. I checked my map and found I could take *La Tour de Val d'Ax* to the gîte at Mérens. That would be good – only ten kilometres and up to about 1400 metres, then down to 700 metres. So, full of enthusiasm and with a real spring in my step, although totally knackered after the day's walk, I flew down the four floors to get a good dinner.

At the small restaurant, sitting outside in the late sunshine and feeling courageous and bold – like a man of the mountains – I cheerfully and confidently asked the waiter for Salade Catalane followed by Tartiflette Royale. Tartiflette Royale is a cheesey thing made with potato and Reblochon cheese – vaguely like an English cheese and potato pie.

You might well imagine my chagrin when the waiter said I couldn't have it. He didn't say it was off, or that they'd run out of Reblochon, or that the Reblochon had run out on them, or even that the computer didn't want me to have it; he just addressed me firmly but politely in French.

"You don't want that – it will be too much for you Monsieur!"

Now I'm a very quiet retiring and peaceful sort of chap – when I'm not in the Pyrénées. Or at least I'm like that when I'm asleep. At the moment I wasn't asleep, so I looked round for a Leki pole with which I could have threatened him, and maybe have used to terrify him into coming round to my point of view concerning the Tartiflette. I couldn't make too much fuss because the restaurant was getting crowded now, and someone had even looked round when I ordered my meal, and had given me a look as if I'd asked for Charles de Gaulle's head on a bed of lettuce. I started to feel as though I'd committed some unpardonable sin, and that the hue and cry might be raised at any moment.

I glanced across the square and imagined them setting up Madame Guillotine. The local press would carry the headline *English Tramp Insults Tartiflette*. In order to make a fine spectacle, I tried to remember the last words from the book *A Tale Of Two Cities* – "*It's a far better thing that I do....*" – so that I could put it in French, but I couldn't get it right. As I sat there silently mouthing some nonsense, I sensed a restlessness next to me and, looking up with a start, I saw that the waiter was still there patiently waiting for my reply.

I didn't say that I'd walked about forty kilometres over hill and dale, and that I reckoned I could eat two Tartiflettes, I meekly accepted his advice.

As it turned out, he was right. The superb Salade Catalane contained anchovies, Serrano ham, chorizo, two large slices of bread with grilled tomato, and a pyramid of lettuce so huge that de Gaulle's head could easily have sat neatly on it. The head would have stayed there until I nudged it with a baguette and caused it to roll off, bouncing to the floor where his large nose would have caught in a knot-hole, while his kepi rolled away between the tables. I could just picture it and the outrage it would cause.

I thanked the waiter for his advice, and decided on a simple omelette nature with chips for the second course.

There were great views from the room of the "Hôtel le Breilh", and feeling very good physically, with neck blisters going down, I slept moderately well that night.

Day 47: Ax-les-Thermes to Mérens
08:15 – 11:45

It was hot and sunny, and I felt awful as soon as I woke up. I didn't want to get out of bed and I seriously considered remaining there and maybe even seeking medical advice.

I had a severe headache, I was coughing, and the soles of my feet were sore after the previous day's long trek on hard road surfaces. I'd drunk some wine last night but not enough to cause this. I couldn't take any petit déjeuner that morning and I was tired after only an hour. I felt dizzy throughout the day, and I was still not right, though a little better when I got to Mérens.

Taking a part of the Tour de Vallée d'Ax that took me off the beaten track to a hamlet called Berduquet, I passed some interesting old big boulder walls and constructions. They looked and felt prehistoric, and there were many sweet chestnuts throughout the heavily wooded region. I had a snickers bar in the deserted and silent woods, and thought how much more confectionery I was eating – all calories burned off within minutes at times.

There now occurred one of the strangest moments of the whole trip. I'd seen no-one so far that day, and I had stopped to admire the peculiar old stonework that seemed so over-sized. I was standing motionless just a few metres from a sharp bend in the track where it disappeared round to the left and I had been still for several minutes, just looking at the walls. I was looking back the way I had come, and was glancing from side to side at the boulder-work that lined the track to get a picture of what it might have looked like when it was new.

The boulders seemed to hold the trees back from the path which was covered in leaf mould, and which was as quiet to walk on as a thick carpet. My back was towards the bend where I was heading. Everything was silent, there was not even any birdsong. As I stood there in the half-light, I suddenly realised that the hairs on my forearms were standing on end, and I could feel what I assume is meant by *hackles rising*. I turned and was fully expecting to be confronted by *something*, but there was nothing there.

As I now stood facing the bend though, most of my hair was now standing on end, and I simply knew that there was an animal of some sort just round the corner. I had no idea what it was, and I was not aware of having heard anything. I just knew there was something there. I took a photograph of the bend as I approached, and quietly turned the corner intending to get another photograph of whatever was there.

Although I believed I was ready for anything, the shock of finding myself face to face with a very large antlered deer was more than a bit unnerving and I just dropped the camera on its wrist strap. The deer snorted and immediately crashed through the undergrowth and took off to the left while I shouted, dived between a couple of boulders, and took flight on the other side of the track. In fact, we both went only a few metres, and turned to look at one another. I'm not sure which of us got the worst shock.

With the realisation that there wasn't really any serious danger – because I hadn't cornered the formidable creature and brought it to bay – I shook my head and returned to the path. I eventually reached the road in a very thoughtful mood – I was most intrigued about the concept of *spirit of place* and the raised levels of awareness that it might inspire.

A reasonably short stretch of road led to Mérens, with its shop, railway station and gîte d'étape. The gîte at Mérens was in a good position, and it was spotlessly clean. I found here, that the strap on my Suunto altimeter was coming apart, and that I couldn't wear it safely – it might have separated, and then it might have fallen off without me hearing it. One of the new boot soles looked as if it was coming unstuck too, although not too serious yet. How many more equipment failures were waiting to happen? I had not tried to cut costs at all when choosing equipment, and I wondered what would have happened if I'd set out with cheaper gear. I bought two or three days food at Mérens – probably too much.

13:15 there was still no guardian at the gîte – though a chap strimming the scrubby grass said there would be no problem. I sat and made plans with the maps. The next two to four days would be critical to finishing. After that there seemed to be gîtes / hotels in abundance. There would be no way to take any sort of detour after Mérens – it would be into the mountains until I got to the other side.

I expected the evening meal to be at 17:00 and was desperately tired to get to bed. Some late walkers, however, meant we didn't eat till 20:15. It was during the three hour wait for dinner, that I devoured a number of books in the luxurious living room of the gîte owner. She'd very kindly invited me to relax in these convivial surroundings with a coffee or two. There were many books on the Pyrénées in general, and on bears and unidentified flying objects in particular. This literary distraction was a fine compensation for the wait.

It was a good meal, and there was some lively table talk. It was still too late to eat for me though, and I felt very negative about the next day. There had been the possibility of illness at home, and I felt like returning on the next train. That could have been 07:45 or 11:00 to Ax, followed by a direct connection at 21:00, overnight, to Paris. I nearly called everything off to return home, and went to bed, very disconcerted and not knowing what to do.

Selected Photographs Andorre

Day 45 – 27 June 09:25
An old shepherd's hut or *Orry* in the mist. Too early to stop for the night.

Day 46 – 28 June 21:47
The bright lights of Ax-les-Thermes.

Day 47 – 29 June 09:18
The Tour de Vallée d'Ax – a lonely passage through a haunting landscape
on the way to Mérens.

Day 47 – 29 June 09:24
Some of the ruins which flank much of the Tour de Vallée d'Ax.

10 Cerdagne, Haute Ariège, Pyrénées-Orientales
Day 48: Mérens to Refuge des Bésines
08:15 – 13:30

Hot, sunny, shade initially, not too bad heat-wise. There had been no early rise like originally planned. I decided to get to Mont Louis about three days distant, and reassess the situation. Hopefully I could get on to Py and wait there for Chris – Canigou might then be possible, and just about the right timing to get to Banyuls-sur-Mer.

At one rest place by a small pool with no obvious source of water flowing in, I felt very competent after searching till I found the spring just below some grass and healthily trickling over some stones before quietly flowing into the pool. It was rewarding to fill the water bottles from such a little-used but pristine source.

A sign at one place along the trail indicated a time of five and a half hours from one cabin in the woods, to another cabin further on. I just beat that time in spite of a couple of stops. The Refuge des Bésines turned out to be guarded, and meals / drinks were available. There were fifty places. Castle said it was a five person cabanne. This referred in fact to another one nearby. My food lugging was totally unnecessary and I'd ended up cooking for myself purely to reduce my pack weight, while twenty five randonneurs were having plat du jour and a party next door. I felt fed-up and left out.

Later on I spent some time just sitting on the balcony contemplating the 2842 metre high Pic Pedros, and feeling part of the elite – I had earlier passed three other walkers who had left Mérens an hour before me, and I'd cried out a hearty *Bon Courage* as I went past. It was during this period of unashamed self-congratulation that some *real* crag hoppers of various ages arrived – some were even grey-haired.

Some of this *really* elite group had strategic flannel bits scattered over their bodies, and one had a very impressive knee support / strengthener with a hole for the kneecap, and with adjustable straps. It would be worth having a bad knee just to be able to wear such a magnificent contraption.

Wait a minute, I thought, I *have* got a bad knee, and I wondered if I could get one somewhere.

Others wore various styles of shorts, some with rolled up legs and some with rolled down waistbands to reveal designer underwear belts – the latter adonis was a grey-haired fellow who looked like a cross between Stan Laurel and Postman Pat. They all looked as if they should be on the catwalk not a mountain walk.

I suddenly felt very fat and weak.

After various consumptions of beer and Perrier, Postman Pat was off to hop more crags – everyone seemed very reverential and deferential towards him. I wondered if he was famous. I'd earlier asked him very clearly where he'd come from today, and he proceeded to show me all the peaks he'd hopped, and to describe all the unmarked escarpments he'd traversed during the last week. He never did say where he'd started *that* day, like I'd asked, and he scoffed at the GR10. I thought he was a bit of a toad. He had all sorts of things dangling from his kit – and flannel carefully intertwined with his sleeveless vest. What a poser, though I have to say I did begin to wonder if I could find some bits of flannel to attach to the straps of the rucksack so I could do some posing myself.

After Postman Pat continued on his rounds, I talked with a man named Jean-Pierre who I'd already met at Mérens. I expected to maybe walk with him some of the following day, or at least meet up with him again later at lac Bouillouses. A Dutch couple, Jaap and Cecille, also became part of what was to become another band of *good companions* for a small part of my life. Jaap and Cecille recommended the GR5 from Holland to Italy as another rewarding walk, and I filed it away as maybe a retirement project.

As I sun-bathed on the terrace during the afternoon with a demi-pichet of rouge, (at least it should be absorbed by tomorrow), I dropped one of my exposed films through a gap in the slats of the balcony. To my horror it hit the refuge's donkey who was underneath at that moment, bounced off, and I watched it roll a little way down a slope. The donkey had also watched it go, and slowly went after it. I thought it was going to eat it, and just managed to get down the steps and beat the beast to it. I almost lost ten per cent or so of my evidence, and realised at that time, just how irreplaceable were my photographs and log.

Later that afternoon, comparing logs with Jean-Pierre, it turned out that he had enquired about the Hourquette d'Arre on 31st May, the day before I went over it in shirtsleeves, with a bad knee and a broken boot. He was told it was impassable, even with ice pick and crampons, and dangerous. He took a taxi round it.

I found out the following year, in an email from Klaus, that he too had left Gabas that same day – he was only a day or so in front of me – on the way to the Hourquette, but that he had to turn back after getting hopelessly lost in the woods that were so badly disfigured by logging. He told me that he finally got back to the hotel in Gabas, from where he'd started that morning, at 23:00 and totally exhausted. Klaus was a very strong walker.

I felt very satisfied with this confirmation of the nightmare that was the Hourquette d'Arre on the 1st June, not at the expense of my friends' problems, of course, and I can honestly say that it was one of the most exhilarating experiences of my life.

It had almost been the last.

Day 49: Refuge des Bésines to Refuge du Lac des Bouillouses
07:15 – 12:45

Leaving the Refuge des Bésines would lead to the crossing from the Ariège to the département of the Pyrénées-Orientales – and this had a Mediterranean coastline.

The overall nature of this day was hot and sunny, washed with a pleasant wind, but always under a deceptively burning sun. In spite of several five or ten minute breaks I knocked a quarter of an hour off Castle's time. I took a series of photographs during the entire day to capture the changing nature of the route. I realised that I should have kept the camera constantly accessible like this on all the days. Many sights that were missed because of difficult terrain or threatening circumstances might otherwise have been recorded.

It was a misty start, sun in face, for the first hour or so that was spent climbing up the easterly rocky valley alongside a small river. Snowfields occurred every so often, but were not too serious. I was bounding along until about one kilometre from the day's end – fatigue came so quickly it took me completely by surprise, and I slowed down considerably during the last few kilometres. On reaching the refuge I had to wait about for two to three hours before I got access to the chambre.

At 16:45, showered and spruced up, the wait for the evening meal began. In these conditions it can be difficult to not drink continually – coffee, Orangina, beer, Perrier. For me, the purchase and consumption of drinks becomes compulsive and ritualistic. It's a sort of therapy – like any other sort of acquisitive salve. Some people collect stamps, porcelain figurines, or beer mats. I was collecting any sort of in-the-mouth, get-ready-for-dinner experience.

To help pass the time I'd usually study the accommodation prospects and distances for the next stages, and consider how I would ensure the ability to return home about the 20th July for Erika's graduation ceremony that was to take place on the 25th. It looked like Chris might be able to get to Arles-sur-Tech where I would then collect him.

The Bouillouses approach had been different to any terrain I'd yet seen – it was sandy underfoot during the final few hundred metres. There was a strong smell of pine resin, and the hot, dry air, with the brilliant blue lac under an azure sky, had a very Mediterranean feel.

Soup, pancakes with béchamel sauce, good boeuf bourguignon with rice, fruit salad. Great pleasant mealtime chatting with Jean-Pierre, Jaap, and Cecile; and a few other guests.

Bouillouses is a very pleasant, although a rather touristy area, with a good gîte and a hotel nearby as well. It's probably badly crowded in the high season. There was a regular bus in the area – they call it a navette. This is a full-sized coach, and it arrives from local towns about once an hour. I never saw more than four or five people on it each time, and I thought what a waste and unnecessary intrusion it was, although it's difficult to estimate the demand for travel in such a remote area – one which yet has an unpredictable high throughput of itinerants such as myself.

Day 50: Refuge du Lac des Bouillouses to Planès
07:50 – 13:00

Yet again it was hot and sunny, with some shade, but I was still badly overheated by the time I arrived at Planès. Months later, I can clearly recall taking my boots off as soon as I got to the gîte, and padding about bare-foot, in ecstasy. Earlier in the day, I'd stopped for coke and coffee at Col de la Perche just below the spot where the Train Jaune crossed the road. The Train Jaune is a small gauge train that runs across the Cerdagne plateau. It's a tourist attraction, but is also a serious addition to the transport infrastructure of the region, providing a link between the many scattered communities of the plateau.

The walking through woods was level and easy, but it was much hotter on any open roads. There was an interesting old Roman Voie (trackway) between Col de la Perche and La Cabanasse. Which was first I wondered, the Romans or the GR10? – and how many other parts can be dated to the Roman era or earlier?

I believed that the many disjoint tracks of the modern GR10 were prehistoric – no-one in their right mind would be up here by choice if the lower plains were habitable. The Cerdagne Plateau had an odd feel to it, and it was difficult to believe it was so high up in the mountains. It was a large, affluent, and wide open area, more like the open plains down at sea level where commerce is more practical. I hadn't seen such low and distant horizons for many weeks

The small village of Old Planès was about 300 metres across a small valley from the gîte, Le Malaza, and it certainly looked like an old strategic settlement between France and Spain.

An enormous key was available at the gîte, and this gave access to an old 11th century church, that was tiny and unadorned on the inside, and which had incredibly thick walls. Crucifixes in the churchyard were adorned with fruit and vines (part of the iron casting) although they looked recent compared to those at Sainte-Engrâce.

Gwen – a lone American walker who was taking a circular tour, not the GR10, was very interested. I gave her details of the book that a friend had written about, among other things, the development and spread of Christian-like religions from antiquity, and the hypothesis that the Eucharist, sun worship, and the dying and rising god, are all eternal concepts, and not the property of any one religion. Such ideas didn't seem at all far-fetched in the Pyrénées.

Jean-Pierre arrived after visiting Mont Louis by bus from Bouillouses, and then walking to Planès during the afternoon. I had earlier thought he was unwise, but he was very lucky, it turned out to be overcast, so walking was cooler. I'd reserved places for him, Jaap and Cecille, and told the patronne that they'd all be eating. To my surprise, Jean-Pierre produced a series of packages he'd bought in Mont Louis, and made himself an impressive steak tartare. In the end only I ate the meal provided by the patronne! Fortunately, she said ...*pas domage* (never mind). A machine wash here for FFr20 was, again, reasonable value – the last clothes wash had been at Aulus, and my socks especially were getting dangerous.

I spoke with my eldest son Jamie, and it was strange to think there was only another week or so of walking. I decided to cut Castle's distances to avoid afternoon walking in the PO (Pyrénées-Orientales).

The meal at Le Malaza was the best meal yet – potage, porc casserole with petit champignons, and some not-so-small forestières mushrooms, superb lettuce and tomato salade with brie, finished off by a fresh fruit salad. A demi pichet of wine of course.

Conversation during the meal revolved around the area of Planès and Canigou, and I heard with interest about an aircraft graveyard near Canigou. This had developed over the years, because of massive iron deposits. They caused the deflection of compasses, and navigational errors that led to aircraft colliding with the mountain in bad visibility.

For the walker and hill-rambler, this is an excellent area, and is open in winter for ballades aux raquettes (walks wearing snow-shoes). It would make a great winter break – Le Train Jaune runs in winter to shuttle skiers and walkers in and out. I phoned Lesley later but the news was depressing – her gran had just died.

Day 51: Planès to Refuge du Ras de la Carança
06:45 – 14:30

It had been a hot, exhausting, and horrible ascent to Col Mitja.

I awoke at about 05:00 after a bad night with very little sleep, although it was an excellent gîte. There were security lights in the bedrooms indicating the emergency exits (Sortie), but they seemed far brighter than necessary and I had found them a distraction even with closed eyes. In addition, because it had been so hot during the night, sleep had been elusive anyway.

There was a good serve-yourself petit déjeuner, and we were off early – four of us in company at first. Jean-Pierre and I later separated from the others – he was great company, and we had a compatible pace. He was ex-army, sixty-ish, retired, and went on all sorts of expeditions to remote places like the empty quarter in Morocco.

At about 10:00 we stopped for a snack at the Refuge de l'Orry. It was on a plateau with a fine view over wooded slopes and rugged mountain tops. This was just after I'd stopped to take a photograph of another old Orry, a primitive sort of stone-built igloo. This larger refuge was still occupied by four young French – three men and a girl. We might have considered spending the night here – the four of us were still together at that time.

Jean-Pierre and myself had left Jaap and Cecille behind after that, and we stopped again at Col Mitja for soup and a snack at yet another old Orry just up from the Col. I noticed that there was an old mouldy mattress inside this even older Orry, not the place to spend a night by choice. Jaap and Cecille passed below us during that second stop, and so they arrived at the Refuge du Ras de la Carança before us.

As we were descending towards this final refuge, an orage started on the surrounding peaks. An orage in the mountains is something to behold. We barely got into the refuge just as it started. For about half an hour there was a deluge like nothing I'd seen before.

Demi pension was FFr130, and the W.C. was a hole in the ground in a wooden shed 100 metres across a field. This was surprisingly hygienic and acceptable, and I was reminded of a tale told me by Old Joe, a sadly departed resident of our village back home. Joe's old school had a dilapidated outside loo, and one day the School Inspector had visited the school, and had also visited the loo. While he was seated inside, Joe and his friends had gathered a bunch of nettles, and thrust them up through the tattered base of the old wooden enclosure. I carefully checked the base of the loo at the refuge, and made sure there was no nettle patch nearby. The bathroom was the nearby stream.

15:30 and it was getting chilly – enough to bring out the fleece. There was of course no electricity, and the refuge after dark was lit by candles. The guardian's kitchen was gas-fired, and as elsewhere, everything was either brought in by helicopter or donkey. No leaving rubbish. Food could be cooked on an open fire in the hearth. This was lit because of the cold. There was a group of walkers cooking at this log-burning hearth with an enormous, soot-blackened, cast-iron *marmite* or pot. This was the best evening yet, with a continuous supply of candles and wine. The refuge was packed – there was a ten strong party of twelve to thirteen year olds with their leaders, and in the group to which I was immediately attached, there were a couple of Belgians – René and Eddy, both forty-ish, and a local fellow named Manu, who was somewhat younger. The conversation was intense, and covered all conceivable subjects. René had given up the rat race, he'd worked in some financial context, and now made roof trusses. Manu used entirely traditional walking / wearing gear and slept outside on the porch rather than in the fug of a dormitory. He was very fervently for local traditions, language, and culture. A really likeable fellow. He's one of tomorrow's real mountain men. (He's really that now.) I fortunately took a photograph of all three. The dortoir was packed, steamy, and echoed to multiple snore sources and children coughing. At one dark moment during the night there was a child's wakening nightmare scream, as some ravenous ogre or mountain troll pursued it with a knife and fork, and a bottle of tomato ketchup no doubt.

Then there was Mr. Bean. This, regrettably English, chap had caused me to have to move from the spot I'd originally chosen for my sleeping bag. Jean-Pierre and I had staked our claims and rolled out our bags when the dortoir was virtually empty. Mr. Bean had subsequently positioned his bag on my spot, and was now in it, with just his nose poking out like a partly cooked pork sausage. He had left me a strip of mattress about six inches wide. I looked at him and considered pulling his sleeping bag drawstring tight so he couldn't get out. With Jean-Pierre's assistance I could then have got him, squirming like a caterpillar no doubt, to the window, and we could have ejected him. The smoothly-tiled roof just below the dormer window sloped gently down, and he would have ended up undamaged and unpunctured in the gîte donkey's pile of straw.

Continuing this exquisite imagined revenge, I saw Jean-Pierre and myself run to the heavy steel door of the dortoir, and rush downstairs before The Bean could escape. He would have to eat his way out of the bag, because when I'd pulled the draw-string tight, I'd quickly tied a granny-knot in it, so that he was now so tightly-trussed, in my mind, that he wasn't going to get out any other way. Next, he was hoisted onto our shoulders and carried to the stream. He bit Jean-Pierre twice on the way, and that was through his quilted sac. He obviously had good teeth. The final punishment was that he was lowered carefully into the edge of the stream, sausage uppermost so he wouldn't drown, and launched. He rotated slowly in the current till his feet pointed downstream, moved out into the main flow humming *Rule Britannia*, and getting under weigh, went with a rush through a small set of rapids, on his way back to the Atlantic. This was greeted by a round of applause from the other walkers. We were heroes.

Dragged back to reality in the dortoir, I could see that Jean-Pierre clearly had the same idea although he was just too polite to say so. He contented himself by moving his bag to make room for me to reposition mine. Jean-Pierre was pretty cool. He seemed fascinated by Mr. Bean, and later told me he'd had a *very strange conversation* with the fellow earlier on the trail at Aulus.

I contented myself with the statement to this Bean-like fellow that if he would care to take the *whole* of my original position, that there might then be room for all three of us. By this time he'd shifted his head within the gloom of his bag, and his tightly shut eyes had also become visible like two compressed walnuts. With the misshapen sausage between them, it was quite a distasteful sight. He didn't answer. He wasn't asleep.

When this fellow had arrived his first question had been wearisome.

"Where's the real W.C. ?"

The hole in the ground was good enough for the rest of us, but he wanted something else. He also said, peevishly, that if it rained next day he was going home. Unfortunately it was fine during the morning, so he's probably still within range. I thought that he'd be better off walking on a treadmill in his bathroom at home, than on the GR10.

René and Eddy, the two Belgians, told me that they come to the Pyrénées every year, and that they just go off onto the HRP (Haute Route Pyrénéenne or High Level Route). That high-level equivalent of the GR10 winds back and forth across the Franco-Spanish frontier; there are few food shops but it has a far superior natural grandeur. I'd already walked bits of it, and would do more later. They would also divert off onto any track that appealed, and frequently got lost half intentionally so they had to compass out of it until they hit something recognisable. They were real pioneering types, and I felt humbled.

There was an appealing and intelligent berger's puppy at the refuge. This little fellow would sit and watch newcomers arrive, intently studying the face and demeanour of the latest arrivals. His ears were constantly changing direction as he took everything in. He also made a great show of wrestling with a plastic sack at one point.

Day 52: Refuge du Ras de la Carança to Mantet
07:30 – 12:00

I didn't sleep well – again. Not surprising given the content of the dortoir. There was a chummy breakfast after washing in the stream. Goodbyes to René, Eddy and Manu – great company. They were all going home. So many times I had had short encounters with some great guys.

It was a deceptive day, shady and windy. We were at 1830 metres on leaving the Refuge du Ras de la Carança, then it was up to 2320 metres at 10:00 (Col del Pal), finally down to Mantet at about 1620 metres, but not before another final climb into the village of Mantet itself. There had also been some ascent and descent between Carança and Col del Pal. I found this constant undulation tiring, and I'd had enough by Mantet. The undulation is a common criticism by many walkers – but then how can you walk a mountain trail without it? Py was only about two hours away, and only about 100 metres ascent. I didn't like the look of the weather but Jean-Pierre went on regardless; I stopped at the Cheval Promenades gîte d'étape which is at the highest part of Mantet. Fifteen minutes later the heavens opened. Jean-Pierre had a good cape fortunately, but he's as tough as old leather anyway.

The gîte people were young-ish and well into Mongolian / Nomadic horsemanship. There were lots of pictures, furniture, clothes, and artefacts of all sorts lying about in the gîte, some of it in glass show-cases; and outside, there was a complete Mongolian tent made of animal skins with a radio playing inside. I was told I could look inside, and that the radio was to give the impression that someone was in there. It was sumptuous inside, with drapes, rugs and solid furniture, – and a faint musky incense hung on the air. What escapism was at work here? Overall, the place had a very rural, bohemian atmosphere, though the chambre and bathroom etc. were very clean and totally modern.

Another Frenchman from the Carança refuge arrived with a Jack Russell, and he wanted to use the same two bed room as me. I addressed him and the dog in a very friendly manner and questioningly rather than with any hostility.

"... Not with the dog?"

He then replied with such an injured expression that the dear little dog was his only companion. I almost wept, but he was offered a separate bed on the landing. I'd even offered to let him and his companion have the room, and said I didn't mind at all, but that I just didn't want to sleep in a room with a dog – any dog. It might snore, I pointed out, trying to lighten the atmosphere. We then sat in the communal room without speaking, and I later saw him leave with his bag and the dog. I felt like the innkeeper at Nazareth on Christmas day. He had, though, been carrying on at Carança in a very self-righteous way, so I thought good riddance.

The patronne at the gîte was as welcoming as Genghis Khan – I thought she might have been a reincarnation – that would explain the Mongolian fetish. Jean-Pierre and I had got a cold reception when we'd earlier enquired about accommodation and the possibility of eating our own food with their drinks in the deserted outside seating area at another small auberge in Mantet. It was very remote and there were no other customers, but nevertheless Jean-Pierre was told *Non!* he couldn't eat his choucroute (snack) with their drink.

René had recommended the higher gîte, and Castle says Mantet is popular with walkers. I think it's an inhospitable place.

I asked to buy a small quantity of coffee, and got two sachets of Chicoree Café that represented themselves as a mixture of coffee and chicory – sixty percent to forty percent. I paid her two Francs and it was awful – I don't believe either the sixty or the forty was coffee. I couldn't believe that René had recommended this place. We should have investigated the other gîte as well. The advantage here, is that it's 100 metres higher than the rest of Mantet, and that means less ascent tomorrow, and that can only be good.

The Fromagerie, a dairy farm with bells and whistles, that Jean-Pierre and I had visited at midday after we were turned away from the first auberge, had been excellent. Bottles of fresh local apple juice, fromage du brèbis (sheep's milk cheese), tomatoes, onions, bread, apricots, all grown or made on the farm. We had a lively talk with the berger / fermier and his wife. This Fromagerie is the only pleasant memory I have of Mantet.

Jaap and Cecille were also at this gîte – Jaap had gone for a run because he hadn't had enough physical exercise during the day – there's no hope for me among these types. He carries most of the gear for them both – a huge sack, and I think there may be another traveller in it who's shy in the company of foreigners.

Jean-Pierre's probably in Py by now, I thought, – I'm not staying in Mantet any longer than necessary.

While waiting for dinnertime, I was told that it might be possible to eat at the gîte, although there was no indication of the facts on which this possibility depended. During this period of suspense, I watched some blacksmiths *doing* the horses, and from the horses' temperament it looked like some of them were still being broken in – kicking and whinnying. A méchant (naughty) black stallion being led to the smith got very excited. The owners were hitting it with swats and a knotted rope, and kicking it, and yanking hard at its tethers. What sort of place is this? If they like horses what do they do to their enemies – I think I'll put a chair against the door tonight.

The presence of mounds of horse manure was of course a beacon to flies – they were everywhere.

My electronic compass that was a feature of the Suunto wrist machine had gone unserviceable today – it had indicated NE all the time, and the heading wasn't changing properly – it said 34 degrees in all directions. I had to go through the calibration procedure three or four times to get it back to normal. Luckily I hadn't needed to use the compass today, or else I could have ended up in the aircraft graveyard, since there was no doubt in my mind that the local magnetic aberrations were the cause. At no other time during the adventure did I need to re-calibrate. My other orienteering compass could also have been way out at times, but I wouldn't have noticed it or known, (unless I'd used it and got lost), and the effect wouldn't have been persistent like the electronic mechanism.

At 18:30 a ceremonial and symbolic column of white smoke was generated from the kitchen to announce to the world that they'd reached a decision. It was finally announced that there would be no food at the gîte.

What a surprise. I then enquired about a place called La Bouf'tic, an auberge in the village. This was the one that had refused Jean-Pierre the right to eat a sandwich with one of their drinks in the garden. I wasn't keen, and walked all over the village looking for the splendid restaurant referred to by Castle, and run by a man nicknamed El Tupi (Strong Fermented Cheese!). If not that, then at least a more inspiring hostelry would have done, but there was nothing. The meal at La Bouf'tic was very mediocre. A group of young French that I had encountered earlier were also there. We had some pleasant badinage, their holiday was almost finished. When I enquired of la patronne about El Tupi, I got some sort of evasive answer and the impression that he'd simply *gone away.*

It remained a mystery.

Maybe Mantet had just been having a bad day, or maybe I was – I'd certainly had enough bad days recently. Anyway, it got the thumbs down from me – maybe El Tupi had come to the same conclusion.

Cerdagne, Haute Ariège, Pyrénées-Orientales

Selected Photographs Cerdagne

Day 48 – 30 June 09:56
On the way to the Porteille Des Bésines

Day 48 – 30 June 13:48
Dropping down to the Refuge des Bésines.

Day 49 – 01 July 07:32
Heading up the valley from the Refuge des Bésines, into the rising sun.

Day 49 – 01 July 07:32 (same time as above)
The view back towards the Refuge des Bésines. It's in there somewhere.

Day 49 – 01 July 08:30
One and a quarter hours after leaving, and well above the tree line.
Looking back, the Refuge des Bésines is now completely submerged in a
sea of mist.

Day 49 – 01 July 11:55
The brilliantly azure Lac des Bouillouses is in sight.

Day 52 – 04 July 09:43
The way forward to Mantet.

11   Canigou, Pyrénées-Orientales
     Day 53: Mantet to Refuge de Mariailles
     07:30 – 13:45

Not too hot, but an exhausting day, although short. Maybe I'm getting soft again I thought.

At the start of that day it rained for about five minutes just before I was ready to leave, but I knew I had to get away from that dreadful place even if it started snowing.

Castle says this section is neither a long nor a particularly inspiring day. I found it wickedly deceptive, with ascents / descents / ascents, and my particularly disliked 600 metres ascent at the end of the day. This undulation went as follows: 1650 metres at Mantet, 1760 metres at Col de Mantet, down to 950 metres, back up to 1125 metres at the Col de Jou, and finally up to 1700 metres at the Refuge de Mariailles.

Fortunately there was lots of shade and it was not too hot. Flies were a menace throughout the day, and my attempts to swat or repel them were exhausting, both physically and mentally – terrible. However violently I flapped my arms about, waved with my hat, or whirled the Leki poles, the flies just stayed in a cloud, and they would land on any exposed skin whenever there was a lull in my activity. I discovered the trick of dipping my hat in the river – the soaking head cover is a great coolant – heat seemed to be drawn from the head as the water evaporated. I wished I'd tried it earlier.

The sour face of Mantet was followed at Py by an early morning *yesterday's coffee* – you know the sort – black as pitch and of a similar consistency, served from a heat-resistant glass jug with as much condensation on the inside as there was coffee. The jug crackled menacingly as le patron, fag dangling dangerously over the cup, brandished it at me. It tasted more like creosote than coffee and I wondered if they mined it locally. This local delicacy cost FFr16 – a bit steep – and I wished I was back in Mantet. At least they claimed some sort of percentage for the coffee content.

Attempting to buy provisions led to a wrangle over FFr2. I dug my heels in and insisted on a recount. The result was another FFr2 error, but this time in my favour. Served him right. You can take Mantet and Py and bury them. Maybe I just hit on the wrong people, but it was the first time I had any grouse against the locals – everywhere else had been trés gentille. Later on I managed some prolonged spurts of walking / ascending in spite of fatigue, and thought my stamina was definitely improving. This was great, but I thought I probably needed another ten weeks to get really fit.

The summit of Mount Canigou was only about eight kilometres sentier (footpath) distance at the day's end, and weather permitting, I believed I should be there the next midday. Some way into the trail I stopped and chatted with a Dutch girl, Nicoline, who was going east to west, and who told me about her problem the previous year finding drinking water between Arles sur Tech and Las Isllas. There wasn't any. I was already aware of the nastiness of that stretch, but she had been forced to give up the year before, because of it. She told me about a new gîte at 661 metres – at a junction about two and a half kilometres after the Col de Paracolls. At the time of our meeting she was on her way to stay with friends at Planès, and I said there was a great gîte there. As it happened, that was where she was bound, and they were her friends. I sent best wishes to la patronne who had been so trés gentille, and compliments again on the food that had been some of the best so far.

I later spoke with many people who had stopped to speak with Nicoline, and who had been advised about the new gîte. I named her the Flying Dutch Girl – she was one of the many pleasant folk who seem to throng the trail.

It was a long end of day drag up to the Refuge. When Jaap and Cecille arrived much later, it seemed that somehow we'd taken different routes; I think I must have taken a longer, unnecessary track.

There was a great bon acceuil, or good welcome, at the Refuge, where a very friendly, young-ish student was standing in for the normal guardienne. It was totally opposite to Mantet. We sat and drank wine and talked about college life in Toulouse, and the bustling city, that shines pink in the setting sun (so I've been told).

Later that evening there was great trouble with the repas. It was undercooked chicken – red inside. After being re-cooked it was still red, and everyone was concerned. I went into the kitchen and helped sort it out. She was new to this sort of catering and was worried that the guardienne would be cross when she returned later. After some high-temperature sterilisation techniques, and the re-submission of the meal to the waiting throng, we were all sworn to secrecy.

We had a very good vegetable soup, magnificent boudain noir (blood sausage, a bit like an under-cooked black pudding), and the saucissons – merguez – were a fine compensation for the under-cooked chicken. The accompaniment of lentilles and onion, and cheese, followed by purée de pomme (apple sauce) was superb.

There was a lot of joking when I said that I would have the left-over boudain noir for breakfast at 06:00, and the young guardienne made some remark and referred to me as Monsieur l'Anglais – the others loved it – and I referred to her as Mademoiselle la Toulousienne which everyone thought most appropriate. Of these others, two pairs were women, one pair French, the other pair French-Canadian. There were some other walkers as well. It was yet another great mealtime – with lots of badinage – mostly directed against myself and England. If ever there was an occasion where a red coat, white breeches, a white wig and a tricorn hat would have gone down well, that was it.

There was a lot of snoring and grunting in the large mixed dortoir during the short hours that remained till dawn, and when I awoke, it was to the smell of boudain noir being prepared. It was a great way to start the day.

Day 54: Refuge de Mariailles to Refuge Chalet des Cortalets
06:55 – 13:30

It was a clear sky, and not too hot because it was so early. Maybe the boudain noir wasn't such a great way to start the day because I felt very, very tired from the start. There was a short steep climb from the Refuge, then fairly cosy walking to a GR10 / HRP junction. This was the Jasse de Cady, and it was followed by a steady climb to the Porteille de Valmanya at 2591 metres.

We (Jaap, Cecille and I) arrived at the cabanne Arago where I knew Jean-Pierre had intended to spend the night so that he could then get an early start in order to be on top of Mont Canigou as the sun came up.

That would have been a few hours previous. Inside the tiny remote outpost there was a wooden platform for about three people and that was it. A clean looking *source* outside and the silent surrounding mountains completed the picture. It truly was a superb spot.

There was no sign of any recent occupation and no note. A note would have been interesting I thought. Perhaps it might have read:

> *...we fought hard during the night and kept the Orcs at bay.*
> *They are now at the door again though, and I am afeared we*
> *shall not be spared this night.*
> *Now the ground is shaking, and the Orcs appear to be making*
> *way for something larger and darker...*

The surroundings definitely suggested the gates of Mordor, and even some of the names had a certain *ring*.

Some way after Arago, Jaap and Cecille went for the Crête du Barbet via a regular track over a ridge to the south-east, and I went for the North face of the Eiger – that's what it looked like from the stony basin to the south of the formidable looking Mont Canigou.

Mount Canigou (the peak) is actually just off the GR10 – the main Pyrénéan route – and is the principal feature of the wider Canigou Massif.

There was a rocky and barren, winding approach to the base of the south face of Mont Canigou. The formidable mountain towered over the expansive scree-strewn slopes and I quailed. A chimney takes you to the summit, and within that chimney there is a final short stage of real climbing. This chimney is sometimes vertical, always almost so, and although a fall would not generally have been for more than twenty or thirty vertical feet, it would have involved a lot of subsequent rolling, bruising, shouting, and no doubt cursing.

I didn't feel like getting annoyed today so I took a few precautions. I emptied most of my water to lighten the load, and I fastened my Leki poles where I couldn't grab them and start whacking things. There were one or two people about and I didn't want to appear, shall we say, *unstable*. I might have to share a dortoir with them later.

I rearranged the wrist gear so it wouldn't grate on the rock face. I'd taken to wearing the altimeter / computer on the inside of my right wrist so the LCD wouldn't get full sun all the time and that had to change for the moment. I tightened all my clothing and the rucksack straps, then thought a visit behind a rock might be prudent before the climb, so I had to loosen it all again.

Deep breath and off we go.

Apart from some raven harassment – they were too quick for me and I couldn't catch even one although I shouted at them – and after some serious stretching for hand and foot holds I got to the top with no problems. It was very windy on the way up, but it had been pinning me to the rock, and that was very welcome. I knew that I would regret putting the poles out of reach; I could have taught one of those ravens a lesson.

When I finally emerged from the chimney and dragged myself over the lip onto the summit I found at first that the view to the east was very disappointing. I'd expected to get my first sight of the Mediterranean, but there were just banks of cloud way below where I stood. The view to the west however was astounding. For maybe a hundred miles the peaks stretched away into the misty distance – far, far back the way I had come – and looking down I could see the town of Vernet-les-Bains. It was like the view from an aeroplane, and the most spectacular panorama all round that I've ever seen.

There was also a cross decked out with Catalan flags and ribbons, and a substantial orientation table. I couldn't resist phoning a couple of old friends to describe the scene.

Sardines on the summit completed a great sense of well-being, and I felt I could handle any sort of physical challenge – given the time. This was the pinnacle in many ways of the whole adventure.

The descent to the Chalet des Cortalets was fairly quick and uneventful. It was just a seemingly never-ending series of arid zigzags, along and down a not too steep shoulder or ridge, with a family in front going at a terrific rate.

At the Chalet des Cortalets I chatted with the French women couple from the previous day. They were in a car for a brief *se reposer* (short holiday) as she described it, before driving back to Montpelier – about two hours by car. They'd seen Jean-Pierre on the road and he'd asked after me. He'd told them I was a peculiar Anglais because I didn't seem to eat at midday. If he'd been with Ed, Michel and me at Saint-Lizier for lunch about six months ago (it couldn't have only been 12 days) he'd understand why.

The woman told me that Jean-Pierre had got to the summit in the half-light, but that he was more than half-frozen. He couldn't see the Mediterranean and it was so icy that he'd been unable to stay there. It must have been very bad. He'd gone on to Batère which was my destination next day. I'd intended to go back to the summit, lightweight, the following morning to see the dawn, but after hearing about Jean-Pierre's experience I decided not to bother.

The clouds outside began taking on wild shapes around Canigou in the distance, and over a three hour period there was an unbelievably savage weather pattern which I quote below verbatim from the log.

The sequence from 14:00 to 17:00 went as shown on the next page.

14:00 Quiet and sunny, hot and still. Clear blue sky.

15:00 Heavens open from turbulent grey clouds – a deluge that completely marginalised the one at the Refuge du Ras de la Carança. Stair rods would be an inadequate description.

16:00 Almost hurricane force winds, horizontal driving stair rods. A thick, grey, fast-moving duvet of clouds, almost touching the mountain tops. Thunder just beyond our valley, like giants throwing rocks at each other.

17:00 Quiet and sunny, hot and still. Clear blue sky.

If I'd been in the chimney when that weather pattern and rain struck, I doubt very much whether I would be sitting here, writing the log-book, I wrote. I pitied any poor devil unlucky enough to have got his timing wrong that day.

On the walls of the refuge there were pictures of the orientation table being taken to the peak, and an account of the installation and blessing procedure. A motorised wheelbarrow frame used to transport it could be seen going up the mountain track with a jockey guiding it.

The weather in the Pyrénées-Orientales seemed bizarre and unpredictable – or did it? It often seemed generally good a.m., and, when there was likely to be an orage, it would frequently happen an hour or so after midday.

I'd been billeted in the CAF stable (no lights, no loo, no water) but I decided to move into the main building with the others for an extra forty Francs. That gave me my own room and a superb view east – will I see the sea? Settled in the room with my camera at the ready, it turned out that I was to be disappointed for a while longer.

As always there were interesting conversations to be made with fellow adventurers, and that afternoon I talked with Richard – a guy from Swiss Geneva – with whom the Dutch had already travelled. He told me about a French prototype sun concentrator at a place called Odeilho on the Cerdagne Plateau. It sounded fascinating, and somehow seemed to fit in with the spirit of place of that unusual area.

Day 55: Refuge Chalet des Cortalets to Amélie-les-Bains
08:30 – 17:50

At 05:00 I looked out to see if the sea was visible. Everything was clouded over. At 07:15 I took a photograph into the sun, trying however to shade the lens with my hand. I was looking at what could only be the early-morning sunlight reflecting off the coastline or the sea, and I confirmed with la patronne that this was indeed the case. The target was at last in sight; it was a sober moment. Everywhere else the outlook was misty, and what would have been fine views were obscured. That's not so bad I thought, I couldn't complain since I'd already had more than my fair share of fine views.

Today was a long, long descent – over 7000 feet, and even the small ascents were also a pain – if you let the reins go just once on the GR10 you've had it. Descending into the gloom the going was unpleasant. It was shady, cloudy, very misty, and very cold at times. Blown mist was bitterly cold and penetrating in the region stretching from the northwest to the southeast of the Crête du Barbet on the way to Batère.

After about an hour I carried on without Jaap and Cecille, her back had been slowing them down, and I took coffee at Batère where I could have made a very early stop for the night. Feeling refreshed however, I decided to push on to Arles – I was on a roll! I later hoped that Jaap and Cecille didn't go beyond Batère, because her back would have been much worse from the long descent, and they'd have been stuck for accommodation at Arles as I was to find out.

At 16:00 I sat in Arles at a café for about an hour and drank two large beers while watching the local youths cavorting and dodging the police.

At about 17:00, when I thought it was about time to book in at a hotel, I went to find one of the expected selection of hostelries at the end of a tiring day. I found there was only one and that it was full. I tried all sorts of ruses. I tried to look small and said a broom cupboard would do. I think I called it a *salle de brosses*. Po-faced, they told me to hop it.

Which is exactly what I did. I fairly hurtled along the road.

I've been known to do this after a beer or two, and I got to Amélie – about five miles away – in fifty minutes. Now after a 7000 feet descent I thought that was pretty good, so I rewarded myself with a stay at the one-star Central Hôtel, right in the middle of Amélie. It was opposite the Café de Paris where there was lots of noise and bustle – a huge contrast after the mountain silence – but not at all disagreeable.

At 20:40 I was still looking out for Jaap and Cecille – there was still no sign of them and I hoped they had found somewhere to stop the night in good time. I tucked into the first of many splendid meals at this modest-looking hotel restaurant: Salade Catalane, Bolas de Picoulat (Catalan meat balls in a sauce of champignons, échalotes, and haricots blancs), crème caramel, a grand café, and calva to finish. Plus a pichet of rouge of course. FFr70 – about £7 all in!! The value was fantastic but the taste and quality was even better. I thought that I must have fallen in the chimney after all, and gone to heaven. On second thoughts, I reckoned that if that had happened it was more likely that I would have been on the escalator going down to the fiery place below, so it had to be real.

The Maître d'Hôtel was an excellent fellow and a first class chef. I was put in a garret on the troisième étage (4th floor). It was sixty stairs up from the rez-de-chaussée (the ground floor), and I hardly noticed them even carrying the rucksack at the end of the day. I knew things had changed because a second floor room very much earlier in the adventure had corpsed me one evening. The room was really a bit of a hole, with peeling paper and damp patches, but it had its own bathroom, was cheap (I would be able to spend more on food), and it overlooked the action in the main street below and to one side.

I could hear a saxophone being practised in one direction and an accordion being played more proficiently in another. I leaned on the ornate cast-iron rail of my balcony and let the Gallic sights, sounds, and smells embrace me. It was definitely heaven.

There was no-one else on my floor, in fact there was little sign of life in the whole annexe, which was attached to, and fortunately contemporary with, the main hotel building. I hate modern architectural arrogance, so I was pleased to be in something that was almost certainly built during France's Third Republic, and probably during *La Belle Époque* – just before the first world war.

France is now on its Fifth Republic – their third one lasted from their defeat at the hands of the Prussians in 1870 to their next but one conflict with the Bosch which resulted in their defeat by the Germans in 1940. There was, understandably, a bit of uncertainty during the second world war years, and they decided a Fourth one would be good in 1946. The Fifth was declared in 1958 when De Gaulle was invited back as the last prime minister of the Fourth republic. He was brought out of retirement to try and find a solution to the Algerian crisis that had been running since 1954. He was made President late in 1958, but the Algerian problem was only eventually sorted out in 1962.

Having thus disposed of the last three republics, I nipped into a convenient Spar shop just a few metres round the corner, and bought a bottle of Badoit spring water and a carton of 100% Jus d'Orange for comfort. It was during this extravagance that I saw several Catalan-coloured bandanas go past the restaurant, and I decided that we needed a couple – one for Chris and one for me to go with my good old companion and good-luck neck-piece that had accompanied me all the way from the Basque country. In spite of many soakings and washings, it still puts red dye on anything with which it comes into contact. The new Catalan one would have to share neck-space with the Basque one, of course, since there was no chance of a replacement at this stage. I'm not superstitious, but I was still a bit concerned about the sightings of the two three-legged dogs a few days earlier, and the Basque bandanna had, after all, seen a few scrapes since it joined the expedition. I reckoned this gave it a major say in the matter. So, rather than risk changing good-luck charms, I decided I'd have to try and finish the trip festooned with competing national colours. If I could add a French tricolour, and the Spanish colours, I could become a roving ambassador promoting good-will throughout the Pyrénées.

I shouldn't even think it, but the body seemed in good shape, although the foot pads were a bit sore from the long downhill pounding of the previous day which had been followed by the sprint along the road to Amélie. That day, I'd only eaten a snickers bar between the paltry petit déjeuner, (Jean-Pierre would certainly not approve) and the evening's blow-out that had been so very welcome. Just before that feast, I'd managed to get eleven postcards written and posted, and after the meal at about 22:00 it seemed that the best option was to retire to bed, and listen to the revelry outside. Perhaps I'll join in tomorrow evening, I thought sleepily.

In the occasional interludes between the music there was laughter from the street below, and sporadic clunks from some distant section of the ancient plumbing system. With the tall windows to the balcony open the long gauzy lace curtains softly billowed into the room under the caress of a light breeze, and I fell asleep bathed in the reflections of flickering neon lights, and with songs like ...*Viva Éspagna...* echoing round the room. This was a great variation – for a short time at least.

Day 56: Rest at Amélie-les-Bains

Sunday: a.m. sunny, p.m. nuage (cloudy / overcast).

Rained several times during the day – some bouts heavy.

This was a very uninteresting day. I scouted out the sentier start point for the HRP / GR10, identified the Thermes and La Poste, and discovered that I could buy a *maillot* – swimwear – opposite the hotel. If the weather stayed like this day, we'd have no trouble walking the final stages during the afternoon – except for the discomfort, and the constant rustle of waterproofs.

There were lots of apartments and smallish houses for sale in and around Amélie-les-Bains ranging in price from about £10,000 to £35,000 – many retired and second-homers were there for the waters no doubt. It's a very busy town. I decided to assess the Thermes next day.

At 19:00 a depressing orage was completely mitigated by the second gourmet's delights of Amélie. An extract from the log reads as follows:

Salade Vallespir (enormous – Lettuces, radishes, tomatoes, beetroot, white shredded stuff – something rapé I think, saucisse, jambon... more and more... an allotment's worth)

This magnificent salade starter was followed by one of my favourite French dishes – Cassoulet Maison.

Now I've always liked Cassoulet. It suits me. Some people think it's just baked beans with *things* in it.

Fie! I would shout, and *Philistine!* I roundly accuse.

I defy even a Philistine to criticise the Cassoulet Maison at the Hôtel Central in Amélie. The inventory was as follows: Duck, porc, beef, saucisse, haricots (naturally), a dusting of parmesan, and whatever else he added in the way of spice, shallots etc.... I asked if he'd got any piments (chillies), and we compromised on a dash or two of Tabasco since I'd left the chilli powder in my room – again.

I have a sneaking suspicion, from the way the waitress looked at me, that normal procedure would have been to order *either* the salade, *or* the cassoulet, but not both. The meal was enormous – it took three of them to carry it to the table – and I've no idea how I'll manage the sixty stairs tonight.

If I could have got in the cauldron with it I would have willingly given up any idea of the natural baths – the Cassoulet was a much better idea. I'm going to ask if I can have it for breakfast as well. Chris must also have it as soon as he gets here if not sooner. Everyone must have it. I'm going to send some home so they can all have it as well.

I wondered if there could be money to be made from a new religion, based on Cassoulet, and centred here at Amélie-les-Bains. I'd be the High Priest and administer it freely to the poor of the region. There would of course be initiation rites that involved dipping in a great vat of it, and there would be special privileges for the priesthood – as is normal in any fanatical religion. With an effort I stopped the thoughts rushing round my head, and decided that I needed a holiday to get over this excitement. Since I was already on holiday, the next best thing was bed.

Sleep didn't come easily that night, and when it did it was pretty fleeting. I couldn't forget the Cassoulet and it featured in dreams when I was asleep. I woke at about 03:17 and seriously considered creeping down to the kitchen to see if I could find any leftovers from other diners.

It was unforgettable.

Day 57: Rest at Amélie-les-Bains

At 07:30 it was cloudy and this was unusual since it was usually clear first thing. By 10:30 there was a watery sun, and I decided to top up on some of the simple necessities of life. I bought soap, sun cream and earplugs – two pairs. One pair for Chris in case I'm snoring, and one pair for me because someone's always snoring. I had quite a negotiation over the price of ear plugs in a Pharmacie. I lost the argument in one pretentious establishment, and got a much better deal in a smaller, back-street place.

I obtained an horaire de bus (bus timetable), and it seemed straightforward to get to Perpignan where I was going to meet Chris, my younger son. I also tried booking gîtes in advance for two nights, and a hotel at Perthus for another. All this via the tourist office. The proposed accommodation turned out to be either engaged, made no answer, or had no phone! I was invited back après-midi to see what further progress they'd managed. They were very helpful and it was cheaper – i.e. free, and that left even more to spend on food.

Now was the time to make my last attempt to take to the waters of a French spa. During the crossing of the Pyrénées from the Atlantic to the Mediterranean I'd tried several times, and every time I'd been frustrated.

I bought a dashing maillot (swimming trunks) so that I could be properly attired, and after having been made to feel as though I was *lowering the tone* during an attempt to get into a Thermes establishment elsewhere, I had a shave and change of clothing.

I felt as though I was going to an interview.

I approached the Thermes, making a couple of detours to be absolutely certain that *Mister Blair* hadn't secretly followed me from Sainte-Engrâce, and chosen his moment for maximum effect. Emerging from a side street, I swept into the square and without a break in my stride, went through the posh chrome and glass doors in a not too undignified rush so he wouldn't have a chance to follow me in. I marched, in as French a fashion as possible, up to the desk. I put on my best accent and addressed the concierge, in French of course, but more or less as follows.

"Good day my dear, may I take the waters at this admirable establishment?"

I was about to give my moustache a twist for good effect, but remembered that I'd shaved it off a year earlier for a dare.

She answered with a smile, and told me in English of course, that I needed a prescription from the doctor before I could use the Thermes.

Well, this came as a bit of a shock because I felt so fit and healthy, and I thought I didn't look too bad. I turned and looked in a mirror just to one side of the reception desk, on the left, and looked in my eyes, and at my tongue. I wondered if maybe I had eaten too much Cassoulet. I asked her if she thought it was something serious. She laughed hugely at this and said that everyone needed a prescription before they could go into the water. You could look at it, indeed even I could look at it this afternoon, but no-one was going in it without a prescription, and that was that. She wouldn't budge. I wondered if there was a secret password or sign that would do the trick, but instead I settled on an appeal to her sense of charity.

"I've walked 500 miles for this, could I not just put a hand in it?"

She smiled again and replied, very politely but in French this time.

"Non! – c'est absolument impossible."

I noticed that her eyes were not smiling this time, and out of sheer mischievousness, I was just about to ask her if she could help me with a small problem that I'd been having with my phone card since Bagnères-de-Luchon, when I caught a movement in the mirror, and saw what can only be described as a slightly reduced version of the snow-covered Pic du Midi d'Ossau, gliding silently towards us. It had emerged from a ceremonial portal over on the right-hand side of the reception area, and my first thought was that it was on wheels, like something designed to terrify at an old-fashioned ghost train fairground ride.

It was only the hair and a few buttons that gave it away. Mountains don't have hair or buttons, human beings have hair but they usually also have some sort of profile or shape. I was getting confused – this was almost shapeless, but it also had buttons. Whatever was it?

So, this monolith had hair but to the casual observer, no other recognisable human attributes. Logic told me that it couldn't be a mountain with hair, so, given that it also had buttons, albeit stretched to breaking point by the tension in the cloth, and that this suggested clothing, it had to be human. It could have been a gorilla dressed up in a masseurs outfit, for that's what I reckoned the clothing was, but then I thought it might have cause to get in the water, and to do that it would need a prescription. No doctor in his right mind would give a gorilla a prescription, so again the evidence was that it was human. It might have had a special dispensation to get in the water of course, but I reckoned that was a bit unlikely.

The expressions and treatment names I had read at Cauterets came back to me, including Gargarisme, and Pulverisation. Pulverisation was certainly something that this thing would be good at, but what was a Gargarisme? I wondered if that's what the thing itself was – a Gargarisme. The name fitted the appearance, and I shuddered to think that they might be quite common in the Pyrénées around Thermes. A 250 kg Pyrénéan brown bear could probably fit in my armchair at home, but this Gargarisme certainly wouldn't.

I suppose its mother loved it, but I didn't. It would, as they say, have stopped a striking clock, it was so ugly.

"Boris!" I heard someone shout from the end of a long tunnel. It surely couldn't really be a Boris.

"Boris, the gentleman is leaving," said the dragon behind the desk in French. This implied that it had ears, but they weren't visible. The only conclusion was that it had perfected the technique that I had so dismally failed to master. They were perfectly flattened, but more in an attack mode than one of submission. I didn't like it one bit, and left as quickly as possible without giving them the satisfaction that it had become a rout. Even if it had.

When I got outside, and after making certain that nothing else had got outside, I glanced round the square, and sure enough there was a dog not far away. They seemed to be following me everywhere throughout the

Pyrénées. This one just stared at me with its ears pricked, and I wondered if they were all in radio contact. Being pole-less, I had no way of intimidating it without risking a nip, so I contented myself with a *Zo!* (Swiss for what are you looking at?) and then realised that I was being watched curiously by an elderly couple who were trying to get past me to get into the Thermes. I imagined they'd just been to the doctor and been told that the only hope for them was to buy a prescription.

I looked for other establishments, and in each one I got the same explanation. You need a prescription from a doctor, no doubt for some inflated fee. It was a stitch-up, a closed-shop. At least there was a piscine in the town, so I hadn't wasted money on the swimwear. I could have bought a couple of Cassoulet for the price.

Lunch – a tin of sardines, two tomatoes, shallots, a nectarine, pain complet, yoghurt, and finally grapefruit juice. Very healthy.

Back in my hotel room, I was just relaxing and about to take an afternoon nap, when my hair stood on end. I heard from the street below what sounded like an *Ondes Martinot*, that haunting synthesised music sound featured in, among other things, the cult science-fiction and weird-fiction programme, *One Step Beyond*, from the nineteen-sixties. One Step Beyond was similar in content to *The Twilight Zone* which is probably a little better known. I looked across to the Café de Paris, from where the spooky sound emanated, and had difficulty believing my eyes, when I saw that it was a man playing a large wood-saw, that he kept under varying tension, with a violin bow. He was playing for the entertainment of diners at the Café. I stood on the balcony and watched and listened, as he played several tunes with never a missed note. The similarity to the Ondes Martinot, one of the earliest electronic synthesiser instruments, (it was designed in 1928), was uncanny, and when he struck up *The Blue Danube*, I looked up and down the street, fully expecting to see two three-legged dogs waltzing to the tune, a complex manoeuvre given the leg situation. The only oddity however, was a man striding purposefully down one side of the street, carrying a pine rocking-chair, and a fire extinguisher. My thoughts became blurred at this imagery, and I rushed to note it down; maybe the sardines were poisoned, I wrote.

Rechecking at the tourist office, when I was sufficiently recovered, I found they'd managed to reserve gîte d'étape places for the 13th and 14th, but that Perthus still remained to be sorted – tomorrow maybe.

Still totally overcast, most of the day – I hope it means the next few days will be clear.

I sent four maps home – 300 gm – equivalent to a packet of pasta. If the weather stayed like this, Amélie was going to be a real pain for the rest of my wait – Tuesday, Wednesday, and Thursday. To inject some interest, I bought two maps at a more detailed scale and studied these to see if they would help us find water sources in the forthcoming arid sections.

It was getting humid – so maybe a good orage was on the way, and then we might get clear weather. I didn't fancy any local walks where I might get a soaking, and I didn't want to take a bus journey that might give me a view of the sea – that would be false – too soon. I needed to walk to the coast in order to fulfil the terms of the original pact with myself.

In all this grey weather I needed sun again, and at 17:50 Amélie did get some sun. 18:10 saw me hanging around the bus station to see what the bus looked like so I'd recognise it when I needed to go and meet Chris from the airport – that would be the last one to Perpignan on the day in question, so I didn't want to miss it because I didn't know what a bus looked like. I felt pathetic.

I searched unsuccessfully for Catalan bandanas until eventually I managed to follow someone who was wearing one of the type that I'd seen earlier. I hoped to be able to get close enough to read what was on it. They must have known that I was following them, because I'm sure they went round in circles to try and throw me off the scent. When they stopped, I stopped, and gazed in the nearest shop window, watching the quarry out of the corner of my eye. Every time I got near and tried to get a close look at their neck I was greeted by a stony stare. Things were about to come to a head, I could sense it.

I suspected that probably I would be challenged or even led, without realising it, to the Gendarmerie where I would be either seized, or the hue-and-cry would be raised; and the whole of Amélie would then be after me up the GR10. I was considering whether I'd be able to outrun the whole town – I was more familiar with the trail, and many of them were geriatrics after all – when I just managed to see enough to make out that the bandana to which I'd been attracted was no more than an advert for some French holiday club. This was indeed a colossal disappointment.

I checked the bus station and was told that it was FFr44 each way and no saving on a return. Perhaps I could get them to handle the Eurostar bookings, I thought. I looked at the bus excursions, and there was one to visit the Thermes; I hurried away before some sort of death-wish could manifest itself.

There seemed to be W.C.s every 100 metres or so, no doubt to cater for aged visitors. They were a very good idea I thought.

For the evening meal at Hôtel Central again, I sat on the roadside. A family sat right behind me smoking – I hoped it would stop before the food arrived, and did some obvious fanning with my log-book.

Le patron at the Central Hôtel was great, every evening now, he would come over, we'd shake hands, exchange a *ça va?* and have a brief, mostly intelligible conversation. He told me of his time in the army when he was billeted locally. With his comrades he would be dropped off at the coast, with orders to march back to their base not far from Amélie. He loved the area.

Escargots, entrecôte and chips. Very good as expected. Demi bouteille of Côte du Rousillon. They had a pleasant touch that I'd not seen elsewhere, they gave a bowl of ice with the water carafe. Simple but welcome.

21:00 He's back across the road. A very short (4'6"?) round fellow about seventy years old and with a face like a broad bean, though not the same colour. He was wearing a pork pie hat, tweed jacket, and twill trousers. A tourist shop, the Bazar du Vallespir, had earlier on this afternoon been the subject of his wrath. I'm going to call him Gus, because that's what he looked like. I'd earlier watched from the balcony, as the lady owner of the shop gradually forced him out of her premises at about 18:45, some while before I came down to eat. He tried to dodge back in, but she caught him each time and ejected him a little less decorously each time.

Eventually, he stood on the pavement and fairly raved at her. He tried to involve passers-by in this action, pointing into the shop and referring to La Cochizane or some such term. Maybe this is a colloquial form of Cochaine? He caused quite a stir, there were faces at windows, figures on balconies (I was one), heads craning round in the open-air cafés, and people were crossing the road to avoid being implicated. He was absolutely determined to make some point. I don't believe he was drunk, more likely just crackers. At one point he was making a sound like a donkey with its head trapped under a piano, while whirling his arms. It was a hilarious and commendable display for a while, but when he realised the audience had dropped below some threshold known only to himself he slunk off.

Well, as I sit at dinner, he's back again, sidling up and down the road – no trouble yet, but he looks as though he's ready, and that he could launch into another entertainment at any moment.

It's very entertaining overall in a slightly cruel way, there are a lot of oddities in a town that professes cures – possibly miracle cures – and it's just plain touristy in places. Just like right where I'm sitting. In the hotel there are Mr. Beans everywhere, ordinary folk with knee-length woolly socks pulled up high in mid-summer, and people of all shapes and sizes staggering about, dropping spectacles, and knocking things over – it's a series of cameo bedlams. There are even people dressed as walkers but merely lounging about in bars I thought with some embarrassment.

Day 58: Rest at Amélie-les-Bains

I visited the piscine during a sunny spell in the morning, but it turned cloudy in the afternoon, so I only got partial value from my new swim gear. Returning to the hub of all activity, I found that they served an excellent Cold Paris Buffet opposite the hotel, in the Café de Paris. This necessitated a nap in the afternoon, but not before I watched a French comedy war film, followed by the *Thé Dansant* afternoon tea dance at the café – this was a display of the elderly re-asserting themselves, and getting rejuvenated. It was fascinating.

A superb Paella Maison at the Central Hôtel in the evening was the climax of an otherwise uneventful and relatively boring day.

Day 59: Rest at Amélie-les-Bains

It was cloudy all day but at least it was market day in Amélie, and my time spent in the market turned out to provide me with excellent entertainment. Tapas and sangria in a bar on the edge of the market was the kick-off, followed by a brief break to visit the Tourist office to find a map of Perpignan, and to get details of les commerces (businesses) – I wanted to find out how much I could save, off English prices, by buying an off-road motorbike to retrace some of my steps a little more quickly, in the quest for a ramshackle cabin for renovation.

Map and business details in hand, I returned to the bustle, and some free-sampling of Moules à la Catalane in the second market set-up. The first market had by now made way for a second one – an unusual practice I thought.

I first knew I was in for an interesting time when I noticed that Gus was at the market. He did a very good job free-sampling from the Moules stall, and also from the adjacent stall selling sardines on bread, and from any other sweet or savoury tasting facility he could find. He'd have a starter on say, the Moules stall, then take a second course from the sardine stall. He weaselled his way among people so he wouldn't be identified, or so he thought, and he frequently had two unchewed portions sticking out of his mouth, and another in each hand. I'm fairly sure he was building up a reserve stock of sticky mussels in his jacket pocket as well, though he must have ended up eating a lot of pocket-fluff like that I thought. He'd smile and simper as he went forward each time to get his latest piece.

I had a great view of him from where I sat at a café bar table alongside the market and greatly regretted not getting a photograph of him. He was a rogue of the first order, and I wondered if he had been trying to free-sample in the Bazar du Vallespir two days back when he met his match in La Cochizane.

Later, Gus had either moved on to richer pickings or had decided his luck was thinly strung, and I was just enjoying an interesting bottle-conditioned Catalan Beer when the second act of the show began.

A local wild poodle (a dog) arrived, and circled the tables slyly. Now poodles can be pretty fierce and violent in spite of their appearance. This one proceeded to taunt another (dog) that was tethered by a leash to a table leg where some customers at the café next to mine were sitting. The first trauma was caused by a lurch of the tethered dog in response to the taunting. Being tethered to the table, it doesn't require a lot of imagination to predict the outcome. The table shot sideways about a foot or so and a bottle (fortunately empty) on the table fell to the floor and smashed but, horror of horrors, the umbrella or sunshade collapsed – it actually closed and dropped – enfolding an elderly customer who had at that instant leaned forwards to save her drink. This happened in much the same way as a Venus fly trap will take a fly.

There was a muffled shriek from inside the umbrella, the scene made me think of the last squawk of the day of a parrot covered for the night, and then silence. The day was saved by le patron who rushed out, threw an old floor mop like a javelin at the poodle, and released the victim from the over-sized fly trap. She blinked a few times but was generally none the worse for the experience. Something to tell the grandchildren I thought.

The third act was something definitely not to tell the grandchildren. The poodle (it's tempting to call it Gus as well) had retreated to the other side of the square and was giving the previously tethered dog a certain *look*. To avoid further tablequakes the leash at the table was now held by the dog's owner, and this dog was returning the *look*. I sensed trouble. With no further preamble the poodle came skipping across the square, and the dog at the table was unceremoniously mounted right alongside the table. Neither dog appeared to have any shame. Now, I've seen pancakes cooked to order at the table, and various other kebabs and sizzling foods presented on a trolley, or whatever, for the edification of the diner. This was something I didn't want to see at the table – or anywhere else come to that.

The next development was equally unexpected; the dog that was on the leash was then released by the owner, and the two dogs were allowed, and even encouraged by some weak applause, to wander among the tables like a pair of close-coupled minstrels, jerking and wobbling tables, and treading on peoples feet. I was just waiting for someone to come round with a hat for a collection when le patron saved the day for the second time. He rushed out cursing, threw a carafe of water at the poodle, and beat both dogs with a baguette that I assume he was just about to cut for the table. If I'd had my poles with me I would have helped.

Of course this was not the end of the entertainment. The poodle sauvage kept coming back whenever le patron had gone inside. It positively frolicked around the tables, peeing on chair legs, and even scoring a shot or two on peoples' shoes and trouser legs when their attention was diverted. It must have been nearly all bladder beneath its scruffy off-white curls. I was glad I was at another café.

I later walked as far as possible through the Gorges Mandanay. This was a high and sheer-sided, rock-enclosed small river course that arrived from the distant mountainous surroundings, right into the middle of town. The walkable part started at a steel fence that had been built across the gorge, with a gate that could be locked at night. It was a strange, short walk which led, after a few hundred metres, to a dead-end. It wound through a very unkempt ravine, in which was an assortment of old bits of irrigation pipe, and shabby derelict buildings. It was a bizarre mixture of very clean, clear river water, surrounded by a range of rusting industrial archaeology and dilapidated, roofless stone buildings which stank of urine, and were littered with filthy mattresses, empty beer bottles, crushed cans, and semi-bleached cigarette packets – together with various other unmentionable and hideous human throwaways. The whole place was protected by a fence as though it was a shrine. I was relieved when I shut the steel gate behind me, and walked back into town past the Thermes that had rejected me a day or so ago.

The evening meal as always was the salvation of the day – soupe a l'oignon – incredible, wonderful. Faux filet a Roquefort – what a culinary heaven – and in the background I could hear the Charles Trênét song, La Mer, again; but this time it was being sung by a live artist and with the whole café joining in.

Writing this log-book attracts a lot of attention – I wondered if I was becoming a bit of a closet showman. Great live singing opposite – Viva Éspagna – yet again, and a singer with a radio mike was wandering among the crowds. Now it's Valencia – they really like the Spanish *musak* around here.

There were crisp outlines to the wooded hills surrounding Amélie, and the cloud layer looked higher. Perpignan tomorrow – fine maybe.

I watched three men at the table next to mine who had a Chihuahua virtually on the table while they fed it as they ate their own meals, and I noted that the underfoot dog-hazards were bad here. As seems common in France, dog excrement is a big problem in towns, and many of the unobservant multitude, particularly older tourists, had managed to treadle through this foul unnecessary mire, and effortlessly transport it into most public places – cafés, hotels, and shops – maybe even the Thermes.

I was snapped out of this mood of revulsion when I noticed the entertainment compère from across the road was now on my side. I was a little surprised that the radio mike stretched to this side of the street, and he was moving through the throng not twenty metres away – roping people into some sort of chorus – time I was gone.

Day 60: Rest at Amélie-les-Bains

Chris arrives today hooray, and it'll be the last section soon. I was not entirely at ease with the prospect of terminating the experience, and I'd come to accept hardships as an unavoidable part of the experience. Waiting for Chris had had its high spots here, but I was itching to get back on the walk.

Sunny early. Perpignan by 09:30. I visited motorcycle dealers – looking for prices on 600cc bikes. I wanted to revisit the bikeable parts of the GR10, and look for cabins for sale. There seemed to be nowhere in Perpignan to just laze about – there must have been, but I didn't find any. Instead, I walked miles around the town. I met the group from Mantet waiting for a train, and after a chance meeting, I spoke with Jean-Pierre who was also walking towards the station area for a hire car. There was nothing extraordinary about taking the navette to the airport, and I was glad I was only meeting an arrival, instead of departing. I was feeling more and more hooked on being in the Pyrénées. I saw Chris's plane land, and went to wait for him in the arrivals control area.

Almost as soon as he was through landing controls, we realised that the lower section of one of his Leki poles had disappeared. It turned out that they had seen it at Stansted Airport on the floor and ignored it, thinking that it belonged to someone else!

Great meals that night as usual. Vallespir salade each, Faux filet des Herbes de Provence (Chris), Paella Maison again for me.

Day 61: Amélie-les-Bains to Moulin de la Paletta
08:00 – 11:30

It was a pleasant, sunny, but shaded first day's journey, and it was only a short section for both our sakes. For Chris because he was starting, and for me because I was re-starting. Chris did not really need any gradual breaking in. He was very fit and there wasn't enough fat on him to fry an egg.

It was a very easy day and the GR10 deviation at Montalbe d'Amélie was no problem. We got to the gîte early and sunbathed while waiting for the guardienne. We were booked in – it was satisfying to know this on this section of the walk due to the increased volume of walkers. Good salade starter, very poor main course – potatoes, artichoke, over-cooked chicken. Good local speciality – a sort of fromage blanc with their own honey.

Chris swam in their pool and I slept quite a bit during the afternoon. Due to their local honey industry the air was thick with bees on missions between the numerous beehives, and heather and acacia in the area. The gîte at the tiny hamlet of Moulin de la Paletta was the one described to me several days previously by the Flying Dutch Girl.

Selected Photographs Canigou

Day 53 – 05 July 08:59

Crossing La Méridienne Verte which runs through the Paris Observatory.
It was a millennium celebration project, and historically it was a rival to the
Greenwich Meridian which passes through London.

Day 54 – 06 July 08:39
Just beyond the Porteille de Valmanya at 2591 metres on the way to Canigou and the Refuge Chalet des Cortalets.

Day 54 – 06 July 09:56
The Crête du Barbet – centre and a little to the right.

Day 54 – 06 July 11:03
Canigou – Cross top left. A party ascends the chimney left of centre.

Day 54 – 06 July 11:41
The top of the chimney, the Crête du Barbet is at centre and top.
A tiny figure, bent over on a less steep section, is just left of centre and
below the final vertical face.

Day 54 – 06 July 12:28
Vernet les Bains – a long way down.

Day 55 – 07 July 07:25
The unmistakeable glint of the Mediterranean beneath an early sun.
Later, at 08:29, it was time to set off on a 7000 feet descent.

12 Roussillon, Pyrénées-Orientales
Day 62: Moulin de la Paletta to Las Illas
07:00 – 14:30

It was very hot and sunny, but for much of the journey there was mostly good shade. This became known as *The Day Of The Pig*, and *The Day Of The Trip To Spain*. The breakfast was a fine affair, and made up for the previous evening's meal – lots of honey, yoghurt, and almonds that had been marinated for a minimum of two weeks in honey. Le patron explained how he made it himself and swore by it for promoting longevity.

We had some trouble finding the *ballises* which on this stretch were identified by blue circles. We had been advised that these were the markings for a track which led up through woods – we were not on the GR10 at this point. It was made more difficult because the map was confusing in the region of the confluence of a river and a track.

At first we overshot the spot where a small winding path left the more substantial farm track which led away from the gîte. We initially began ascending a path that led up a spine of rocky sparsely wooded mountainside, but the views and compass bearings just did not fit with the map. It was obvious that something was wrong, but not obvious what the solution was. Retracing our steps we found another track that was still not verifiable with certainty, but which we decided to take just to *see what happens*! It soon became apparent from directions and altitude changes that it was about right.

On the way to the Roc de France, we passed some renovations being carried out on a sprawling mess of superb *Mas* farm buildings. The Mas is a regional term for farm buildings with a shallow-pitched roof, usually in terracotta, and more commonly found in Provence – where snow is just about unheard of – some three hundred or so miles to the east. There was a group of youngish people with children who looked as if they'd gone back to a more primitive way of life. The difficulty of course, for most people who would like to try it, is that to do that sort of thing you have to be able to afford it in the first place. We confirmed with these folk that we were on course, and continued on our way with more confidence.

It was somewhat misplaced.

We ended up visiting the Roc de France though we didn't intend to, and we followed the HRP for a way. We had, without beating about the bush, got lost, and blindly went towards higher ground through trees and scrubby undergrowth. We did in fact do quite a bit of bush-beating; and after leaving the tree line, we had to scramble through some awkward bracken that was strewn with boulders, on the ascent to the Roc.

Passing through some of this bracken before the trail disappeared, Chris disturbed an enormous sanglier that was just on the edge of the track. We both heard it grunting and saw the bracken waving and being trampled as it careered away. We were probably very lucky, since it would not have expected to be so closely approached, and I suspected that there was something unusual about the fact that this happened in daylight. If it had been old or injured, and unable to hobble away to safety, it could have given us a lot of trouble.

After the Roc, we took a track from the nearby TV station into Spain. We discovered that we were actually in Spain at the TV station, where a Spanish technician told us (in Spanish) about tracks and a road to the Col that we wanted. It was strange to understand what he was telling us although we didn't speak Spanish. The terminology, gestures, and intonation left very little to doubt.

It was a very rough, bad descent from the Col. There was a lot of conifer forest, and a lot of undulating ground with exposed roots – all the tracks were rough and strewn with stones. Chris fell at one point and bent his last Leki pole, although fortunately it was still usable. There was eventually a long road walk into Las Illas, where every bend that we thought was the last, just led to another.

Arriving fairly exhausted at Las Illas we found there was no-one about. The gîte d'étape, situated in the Old Mairie building or town hall, was obviously full with a big party. We'd reserved places, so what was going on? We had to wait till about 17:30 (that was about three hours) to find out that there was other accommodation in the Guardienne's house / basement, and that this was what we'd been booked into. We had superb meals at a local restaurant – Muscat aperitifs, salade aux magrets (Chris starter), chèvre chaud starter for me. Faux filet for Chris, (poivre verte), confit de canard for me. A litre pichet of vin rouge, calva, and finally crème caramel for me. The day was improving. Chris and I sat just on the outside of some homely family meal-taking, and we enjoyed the simple and undemanding relaxation.

For extra entertainment there was an orage in the early evening before the meal. We luckily took ponchos because we'd expected it, and there was another during the meal. There was literally a river down the street.

After we got back to the gîte there was another orage that lasted all night. The full works.

Another randonneur was going to Banyuls-sur-Mer – all the way – the next day, and he had an 05:00 start. He was gone when we emerged from sleep late at 07:30.

Our plan had been to leave at 07:00 at the latest. It was neither a good start nor an inviting day.

Day 63: Las Illas to Col d'Ouillet
07:50 – 16:00

We dragged ourselves out of the large communal sleeping room after a jus d'orange (bottles that I'd bought from the restaurant the night before), and although it wasn't raining it was definitely thinking about it. We had to be very quiet during all our morning ablutions because there was another family of walkers berthed with us, and they were still sleeping only inches away.

It was grey and windy, and fairly soon it was raining hard; and the wind had increased. Walking in strong wind and driving rain (it was coming from the side – the north more or less) is fine if you tell yourself you're enjoying it. We loved it.

The predominantly level sandy tracks had been washed flat overnight, and any sloping sections that we came across had runnels and rivulets that were being amply maintained by the latest deluge. It was a very sea-shore like environment in places, complete with sand, fresh water pools and lagoons, and a substantial flow of river water making its way to the sea. In the present circumstances the sea was of course rather remote.

There were many managed cork woods on the approach to Perthus, and the stripped tree trunks which had been painted with some sort of protective lotion were bright orange in the rare patches of sunlight. The trees are flayed for their bark to a height of about two metres, but manage to regenerate their spongy skin. It looked agonisingly painful.

Unfortunately the cork forests are only as safe as the market for cork, and with the increasing use of synthetic bungs and screw-tops for wine bottles, cork forests are under threat – particularly in Spain. I wondered if this was because many of the ex-Spanish colonies are in the forefront of this drive to plastic, and whether they used to make up much of the Spanish export market. The French, being more traditional, would be expected to keep their cork forests in good shape.

The general slog to Perthus ended at about 11:30 with a rewarding lunch – charcuterie for Chris, Salade Niçoise for me. As has happened on several occasions I had to remind them that a Niçoise should have anchovies. It was one of their inventions after all, and I was surprised that they so often got it wrong. The anchovies finally came on a separate plate and much ceremony was made over their presentation. I've had to refresh the waiter on what a Niçoise should consist of many times at home as well. Do they think they can get away with something or is it accidental I wondered, as paranoia reared its ugly head again.

We had coke, sangria, and, specially prepared for us since it hadn't been on the menu – maybe they felt guilty about the Niçoise – omelette à jambon. Each. We ordered a portion of frites then found they were included with the omelette anyway. Déjà vu I think. We were totally stuffed and couldn't finish the frites.

During the afternoon we walked well – mainly on roads – and the weather improved considerably. Chris wanted another adventure. I'd already had enough of them for a while, but he continually looked for a shortcut across the zigzags that the road was taking towards the gîte that we could clearly see perched on a cliff way above us. No suitable death-trap presented itself, so we stuck to the road. I knew by experience that this was the best idea, and was relieved to find that he wasn't going to succeed in leading me astray. I wondered if he'd ever come across *Mister Blair*.

There was a mass of bracken, brambles, and unseen sharp rocky cliffs and all sorts of barriers among the dense trees anyway, as we later saw more clearly when we eventually reached the top and looked back down at the way we'd come.

So, to Chris's disappointment but my great relief we got to the gîte the safe way, and were rewarded by fantastic views from the wood-slatted terrace. We sat there sunning, reading (Chris), and writing up the last couple of days' escapades in the logbook. The logbook was never normally more than a few hours out of date, but the last two days of rain and extreme hours, had introduced a delay, the detail of which, was easily overcome later by our joint recollections.

17:45, waiting for food and bed – an early rise the next day was essential, it was almost certainly going to be very hot.

The gîte was full that night, and the family with whom we'd shared the dortoir at Las Illas, arrived late. There was a mild altercation when they were at first told there was no room and turned away. They then impressed upon the guardian, quite rightly, that gîtes weren't supposed to turn anyone away late in the day. They finally got a recently painted room, and were obliged to sleep with the windows and door open all night to avoid a glue-sniffing incident.

Day 64: Col d'Ouillet to Banyuls-sur-Mer

07:00 – 15:00

So this is it, the last day. There was an excellent petit déjeuner, a good start, and immediately afterwards, a horror ascent through woods to get back up to the GR10 that was a few hundred metres higher, and to the east. Well, I thought, you can't expect anything to change when you're crossing a mountain range from west to east, and all the valleys run north to south.

It was shady for most of the early part of the day, but intensely hot as we neared the descent to the coast. Much of the route was undulating as if the mountains wanted a final assault on the will – really rubbing it in.

It was during a steep descent over rocks, that I fell and smashed my analogue watch that I'd had for more than thirty years. Watch glass disintegrated, hands bent and useless, it completed the journey in the darkness of my pocket. This was indeed a grievous injury to what had been, for thirty years, a constant companion.

We were amused at one high point – the Col des Gascons – to watch a French group having a very heated and animated argument about the route. There was also an option here for us. Whether to take a more substantial track – the older GR10 probably – or whether to take a goat track winding up the side of a ridge. Chris and I then had an argument as well, about which route to take. Three of the French went on with their original route which led them back where we'd come from, and one woman went the same way as us, over the higher ridge, (this was Chris's preference as well of course), to where we had a last mountain lunch of saucisse and pain complet under a tree by the side of the road that sloped down towards the unmistakable outskirts of Banyuls-sur-Mer.

It was a hot and dusty, winding approach to the journey's end, on and on, apparently endlessly. A never ending descent through vineyards was how we made our way down to the outskirts of Banyuls-sur-Mer. Eventually we went under a railway bridge, and joined the last road going east. At this time, Chris was hanging back to give me the honour of the completion of an incredible experience, through the town streets, over a low wall, and straight on, down a gently sloping stony beach, and into the blue Mediterranean – both hands of course.

The End

Selected Photographs Rousillon

Day 57 – 09 July 18:50
The view from the Central Hôtel, Amélie les Bains.

Day 63 – 15 July 17:27
The penultimate day – Canigou is just above the cloud and mist on the right, and a very distant Spanish peak is on the left.

Day 63 – 15 July 21:13
The last Pyrénéan sunset of the expedition – seen from the Col d'Ouillet.

Day 64 – 16 July 11:31
Banyuls-sur-Mer – the end in sight.

Day 64 – 16 July 15:04
A ceremonial immersion of the hands – centre.

Day 64 – 16 July 15:05
That's all folks!

Printed in Great Britain
by Amazon